To my beloved Sister ♡

GATHERING IN

COVID-19 Silver Linings

Looking forward to the day when we can once again "gather in" as a clan in the land of our roots!!

XX oo

B.

GATHERING IN

COVID-19 SILVER LININGS

26 NOVA SCOTIA WRITERS, MUSICIANS AND ARTISTS

Copyright © 2020 – Individual contributors of stories, poems, lyrics and works of art retain the copyright to their writing, lyrics and art.
All rights reserved. No part of this book may be reproduced, stored in a retrieval system
or transmitted in any form or by any means – including photocopying or electronic or other reprographic copying
without permission of the author
through WindyWood Publishing,
Nova Scotia.

Issued in print book format:
ISBN-13: 978-1-7753583-9-8
Editing, layout and cover design: Pat Thomas
Graphics optimization: Trevor and Darlene Awalt
Dream Imagine Believe Photography
Bayswater, NS

WindyWood Publishing
372 Highway 3, R.R.#1, Hubbards
Nova Scotia
B0J 1T0

DEDICATION

This book is dedicated to all Nova Scotians who lost loved ones during COVID without sharing final hugs and words of comfort. We know the gaps these people leave behind and how much they are missed.

As well this book is dedicated to those who recognize and cherish some bright moments of inspiration, insight and appreciation during this COVID-19 pandemic.

We appreciate the inspired work by the contributors to this anthology and thank all for sharing in such a personal way.

The hope is that this collection will endure and influence and inspire others to realize and cherish moments with family, friends, creating memories that enrich our lives – even during dark times.

EDITOR'S NOTE

Gathering in contains creative silver linings inspired by defining moments within and through the clouds of isolation and fear and loss that we endure during the COVID-19 pandemic.

As such, *Gathering In* is a compilation of works by twenty-six inspired Nova Scotia writers, poets, spoken-word poets, artists and musicians.

It was a pleasure to work on this anthology with these talented writers.

This collection offers brief glimpses into Nova Scotians' depth, diversity and resilience during tough times – during Nova Scotia's first wave of the COVID-19 pandemic in 2020.

P.A.T.

INTRODUCTION

THE WEIGHT OF COVID-19

July 2020

The entire world staggers under the onslaught of the COVID-19 virus. This coronavirus, undetectable to the naked human eye, has altered life for the whole human race. It seems almost inconceivable that a virus in an animal on the other side of the world should migrate to the human race, and from January to July, 2020, spread to at least 15 million people, with, as yet no known vaccine to help us all.

A world in which there is a "pill for every ill" is shocked beyond belief at the COVID-19 pandemic.

How does one deal with a pandemic that outstrips any other pandemic?

Nova Scotia is blessed with strong leadership. Here, under the consistent and capable leadership of Premier McNeil and Dr. Strang, the virus outbreak is largely controlled with most new cases ascribed to visitors from outside the province. Masks, social distancing and strict personal hygiene, plus the cooperation of our people, have helped to manage and contain the virus.

Many among us have restricted our personal freedoms in the interest of survival and to help our neighbours. A resounding "yes" is heard to the age-old question: Am I my brother's keeper?

Meanwhile, people the world over realize this is a deadly serious matter. The "not me" reaction does not work, and the virus can create a second wave if individuals and nations disregard warnings and act selfishly and recklessly. Especially vulnerable are the aged and infirmed. We cannot carry on as usual, as much as we value our human freedom.

Our self-confident world is shaken and challenged. The *Titanic* was thought to be unsinkable, but that wasn't true. Humans are face to face with how fragile and vulnerable we really are. There is new meaning to Wendell L. Wilkie's "one world," as nations reach out to support each other and for help.

The world has changed: The stock market has dropped, many places of business are shuttered or bankrupt, offices are empty, airlines are grounded, "normal" life has vanished and society conjectures with foreboding, the shape of the future – plus we live with the haunting fear of the second wave. Climate change looms on the horizon but the pandemic is here now, a present threat to human existence.

There is a need for continued restraint, and also for hope and optimism. We have survived famine and floods, the bubonic plague, two world wars in 20 years. Hiroshima has terrified us, and we have battled SARS and AIDS. We hear the adage "this too shall pass" and we try to believe that a new vaccine will be discovered and a better day is ahead.

TED THOMPSON

Ted Thompson is a 92-year-old retired United Church minister. He lives independently in his home in Halifax.

CONTENTS

INTRODUCTION
TED THOMPSON......v

GATHERING IN 1
PHILIP MOSCOVITCH

IS THIS WHAT IT TAKES? 8
ALNOOR RAJAN TALWAR

HOW A FLOCK OF PIGEONS GOT ME THROUGH 14
DEBORAH WASHINGTON

BRING THE SILVER 18
JAN FANCY HULL
    THE LONGEST DAY 19
    I LEFT THE EARTH 21
    FLAGS 22

THE BLUE DRESS 24
HEATHER D. VEINOTTE

INTERMENT DURING A TIME OF PANDEMIC 33
BONNIE L BAIRD

SOMETIMES IT'S TOO MUCH 35
DYLAN B. FASSBENDER

NEW GROWTH (SPRING, 2020) 41
JANET BARKHOUSE

CHASING GLIMMERS 43
BONNIE L. BAIRD

A FRIEND REQUEST FOR PHILIPPE PETIT* 45
CHAD NORMAN

THREE HEARTS + FOUR 47
RUTH ANN ADAMS

HELLO! 51
CHAD NORMAN

PORTALS 52
JENNIE MCGUIRE

RUSTWORKS 57
BEVERLEY MCINNES

WE'VE GOT THIS 61
GLENDA PENNELL & MELANIE DONNELLY

THE CARNIVAL 64
KATHY FRANCE

TEACHINGS OF HENNY PENNY 69
JENNIE MCGUIRE

THE FASCINATING "TRAUMA" OF BEING QUARANTINED!......71
DOROTHY GRANT

THIS TIME THE GOVERNMENT IS GOOD FOR YOU......77
DR. GREGORY V. LOEWEN

NOVA SCOTIA LOCKDOWN......81
CYNTHIA FRENCH

EARTH DAY 2020 84
BARBARA MENZIES

OBLIVION'S WAKE......86
DAVID HUEBERT

WITH LOVE…COMES HOPE......90
ALNOOR RAJAN TALWAR

BLESSINGS ON THE BROKEN ROAD 92
CHAYA GRATTO

A Reading of Clouds* 97
Chad Norman

A Study in Isolation......99
Alnoor Rajan Talwar

Despite It All......101
Catherine A. MacKenzie

Coping with COVID-19 103
Sylvia Lucas

Breathe......109
Bonnie L. Baird

Love Conquers All......112
Mary Anne White

Now Easter Comes 117
Bonnie L Baird

A Long, Long-Term Lockdown......119
Louise Piper

The Gift of Fear 125
Bethana Sullivan

Olygyology 129
Alnoor Rajan Talwar

Survival: Here I Am! 130
Chad Norman – for Nicoleta

100 Days 132
Brent Sedo

Contributor Bios

Ruth Ann Adams......138
Bonnie L. Baird......138
Janet Barkhouse......139
Melanie Donnelly......140
Dylan B. Fassbender......140
Kathy France......141
Cynthia French......142
Dorothy Grant......142
Chaya Gratto......143
David Huebert......144
Jan Fancy Hull......144
Dr. Gregory V. Loewen......145
Sylvia Lucas......146
Catherine A. MacKenzie......146
Jennie McGuire......147
Beverley McInnes......147
Barbara Menzies......148
Philip Moscovitch......149
Chad Norman 150
Glenda Joy Pennell 150
Louise Piper......141
Brent Sedo......151
Bethana Sullivan 152

ALNOOR RAJAN TALWAR......153
HEATHER D. VEINOTTE......153
DEBORAH WASHINGTON......154
MARY ANNE WHITE......155

GATHERING IN
Philip Moscovitch

My visitor is talking about relaxation again.

"Really, relaxation is what we are going for in Qi Gong," he says, as he gently twists his torso, swinging his arms from side to side.

I watch him and mirror the movement, standing on the yoga mat in my office, my chair pushed off to the side.

The visitor's name is Colin Donohoe. He's in Australia, where at some point in the last few years he started recording a series of educational Tai Chi and Qi Gong videos in a park. Unfamiliar bird songs punctuate the movements, people stroll or bike past in the background and there is a steady rumble of airplanes, presumably taking off and coming in to land at a nearby airport.

Remember airplanes? Remember airports?

I swing my arms, then follow Colin into the next move, a slightly different motion now, bringing them up to my chest and letting them float down while I gently bounce through my knees.

"Nice and easy, using the least amount of energy," he says. "Just try to relax your body as much as you can."

Relax. Relax, Phil. Relax.

In early March, I was relaxed. A little worried, yes, but relaxed. My son and I had gone to Tampa for four straight days of hanging out with my father-in-law Peter and his friends, going to ballgames, and generally taking it easy. Mornings, I swam laps in the small pool at the house we'd rented, trying to clear my mind and thinking about the day ahead.

After towelling off one morning, I heard Peter on the phone with his girlfriend, Veronica. Italy was going on lockdown and cases were starting to appear in Florida, but they were a handful, and not in the Tampa area. I gathered Veronica was concerned. I didn't hear her end of the conversation, but at one point Peter snapped, "It has nothing to do with the coronavirus!"

Three days later, we were home. By then I was reading about people in Italy being left to die, and worrying I was going to be one of those triaged out of healthcare when the exponential wave inevitably broke over the shores of Nova Scotia in a few weeks or a month.

After those few days in Florida in early March, there wasn't going to be any relaxing. Not for awhile.

I stood in the kitchen, heart pounding. My body was emptying the dishwasher. I know it was me, but it didn't feel like I was there. I was somewhere deep inside, my consciousness a little pinhole of light hidden away between layers of fear, my body a seeming automaton carrying out these simple movements out of habit.

Bend, grasp dishes, put on shelf, reach down, grasp dishes, put on shelf, bend, pick up cutlery rack, and so on.

Later, going down to the basement to get something from the freezer, my legs felt like they could hardly negotiate the steps. One in front of the other, my body driving forward as I watched from somewhere inside, wondering if I would stay on my feet or fall down the stairs.

Most mornings I would lie in bed alone, sometimes for hours, scrolling and scrolling and scrolling through the bad news on my social media feeds, feeling that wave gathering strength, sure that it was going to soon drown us all. Or at least many of us.

And definitely me.

I started Tai Chi back in January, together with Kent, my other father-in-law (my partner has a biological father and a stepfather). Every Tuesday morning I'd pick him up and we'd drive to a local community centre for our class. Slow-moving Qi Gong movements to warm up, then working our way through what are known as the essential 18 forms. We were just getting a taste of the practice, the slow, meditative moves, the soft power that comes with deliberate movements.

Then I went to Florida; then the Tai Chi classes got cancelled; then everything shut down.

A few weeks later, with the province in lockdown, our Tai Chi instructor emailed his students. He had recorded a video of the warmup practice he led us through at the start of each class. Since we couldn't go to class, we could follow the videos if we wanted to practice at home. More videos followed, each demonstrating a different Tai Chi form, each with its own evocative, poetic name:

Buddha's Warrior Attendant Pounds Mortar, Lazy About Tying Coat, White Goose Spreads Its Wings.

"Do you want to do the Tai Chi together Phil?" Kent asked one day when we were chatting. I've known Kent for more than 30 years. We've gone back-country camping together, we talk books, films and politics. We even used to work together. Since we were locked down, Kent figured we could just call each other, then run through the Tai Chi practice, each watching the video simultaneously from home.

At first it seemed odd to me. I could just do the practice myself. Why would I watch it while having Kent on the phone?

But I said yes.

The first day, we went through our instructor's warmup together. I stood out on the deck (an unseasonably warm early spring day) and watched the video on my phone. At the end of the session, Kent said, "Same time tomorrow?"

"What?" I said. "You want to do this every day?"

"Well, you can have Sunday off if you want," Kent said.

"As we do this movement, you want to stay as relaxed as possible," Colin says.

The movement is called Gathering In. One of the fundamental Qi Gong movements, often used as a bridge between forms. I stand with my feet shoulder-length apart, slight bend in the knees, arms at my side, palms up, then lift the arms and bring them in toward my chest in a circular motion. Hands now face down, then slowly lower down in front of the body while exhaling. Arms out to the side again; breathe in while they slowly rise, gathering energy before once again slowly bringing them down in front of me.

My phone buzzes. I'm expecting to hear from an editor, but I'm learning to ignore the interruptions.

I keep gathering in.

I called Kent again the day after our first online practice. And the day after that. Sometimes he called me. We chatted, some days for half an hour: talking about his bathroom renovation, the number of new COVID-19 cases, the latest announcement from Trudeau, the troubling developments south of the border. We had introspective conversations about racism and complicity. We talked about mundane things like the weather.

Kent lives less than 10 minutes away, but of course we couldn't go visit. Socializing meant weekly Zoom calls with family, walks through the woods to meet friends at a distance (we'd sit on opposite sides of a stream) and our daily Qi Gong practice.

I hardly took any Sundays off either.

Most days we would set up in our offices. "Let me just push my chair out of the way," Kent would say. "Three, two, one, go...." as we both hit PLAY at the same time, my phone sitting on the desk in front of me, the video playing on the monitor.

Arms floating up, crossing overhead, halfway down. Pause, exhale, lift, slowly descend, start over.

The movements were gentle, repetitive and sometimes challenging. There was a comfort knowing Kent was in his office, his chair pushed off to the side like mine, his arms rising and falling at the same time as mine, both of us connected through our practice.

After a week or two, I thought it would be a good idea to find some new routines to follow, for variety. We bookmarked videos by instructors in the US, the UK and Australia. Colin, the Australian instructor, was one of our regulars.

Weeks became months. Lockdown ended, but the state of emergency remained.

Every day, we practiced.

Sometimes my heart still pounds, even as I'm trying to breathe with intention. Sometimes I carry on the practice semi-attentively at best, my mind on the work I need to do later that day. Sometimes, yes, I do pick up my phone and glance at that message from an editor, or the latest comment on my most recent article. Occasionally, I reach forward and flick the mouse so I can see the progress bar at the bottom of the screen. How much longer 'til this ends?

But the Qi Gong has become a mainstay of my daily life now, and so has my daily chat and practice with Kent. One of my anchors. Something grounding amidst all the uncertainty.

Colin stands with his hands folded over his lower belly. I do the same, eyes closed. I drop my hands to my side, open my eyes. Colin's in close-up on the screen now.

"You're probably feeling just as relaxed as I am," he says. "It's a beautiful exercise you can practice anywhere, at any time."

I lean forward and hit STOP before YouTube starts auto-playing the next video.

"Same time tomorrow?" Kent asks over the phone.

Is This What It Takes?
Alnoor Rajan Talwar

Alnoor Rajan Talwar shares this link so you can listen to and read along as he performs his spoken-word poem:
https://www.youtube.com/watch?v=Y1SHow1OlH4

      do you see it?
           do you smell it?
                can you sense it?
it's all around us...
...the foul scent of fear and isolation,
infecting our world
      like the very contagion
        that caused it
                unchecked, it spreads fast
                seeking out the young, the old,
                the weak, the able, the fairest
                and the darkest of hearts
                alike
                regardless of
        colour, creed, race or caste...

...an inclusivity, that humans
  would do well to learn from
     what do we do?   how do we react?
    we isolate
        we adapt
we find things to occupy
        our lives
        we comply,
        we re-invent,
        and continue...
...because, we are human...it's what we do...
              ...if we sat idle,
      the would've, could've and should've thoughts
    are too many
      and so very scary

so, we carry on with precious life as best we can...
  ...we awaken,
      we give thanks,
          seeking new meaning in solitude,
finding solace in nature...
    ...looking for magic and mystery in quietude
    recognizing the beauty that exists...
              ...with every rising sun
        ...in the moonlit and moonless nights
          and in every gust of wind,
losing ourselves in books, movies
          and music...
...searching for some peace
amidst the anxiety and chaos
and,
 in going back to the basics

we re-learn to live and feel
        in order to heal
   the hours seem longer
        and the days blend into one another
        as we continue to ponder
          our unpredictable future
and even though we stand   six feet   apart
in our distancing and forced isolation,
   on the brink of this dark oblivion,
     we remain
        somewhat collected, united and together

but the "truth" is so much more
        than just the crisis at hand…

history shows us that we have good reason…
          to mistrust everything,
           especially one another…
    we pretend to be
  rash
   while treating others like trash
     -we say what we do not mean
     and mean what we do not say
     -we seem to be
  excellent communicators,
but constantly speak in riddles
             -we wear our masks well,
    everyone, everyday, everywhere…
   …so well, that we forget
        who we really are
   and who or, what we can be (for each other)…

the most reasonable act
        would be to set
                all our excuses, facades and differences
        aside

      for, at the very core of humanity,
          lies a common actuality…
      -a shared wisdom…
            …an inherent tendency towards
         peaceful unity
    to help reclaim our sanity
from the ashes of our self-inflicted calamities

i remain in constant awe
of what we are able to accomplish
when we choose to ignore
    our petty differences,
        and come together
         for a common cause,
            for life,
            for humanity,
            for our communities…

        …and as communities,
we have responsibilities…
    …each one of us has a choice
      each one of us has a voice
…it is about how we choose to live…   …with or
without limitations
        and with or without inhibitions

we may fail to see,
but the possibilities
        are quite plenty
and right here, within our midst

sure,
we cannot unhear the things we've heard,
        unsee the things we've seen
              or, undo the things we've done
we cannot help but be
constantly worried
about who or what's lurking
        around the next corner

but then, something happens…
an emergency,
  a calamity that affects
      the whole of humanity
      bringing us face to face with our mortality
     reminding us
        of who we really are and who we can be
and that is when
we rise to the occasion
  and we shine…

       …we hear beyond hearing,
           we look and see what we commonly do not,
               we feel beyond the sense of touch…
        …our souls connect
           we unite
           we fight

...not each other, but together
without
    any financial motivation or
        the violent retaliation
            that we are so used to
                and without the vengeful obsession
            that we are so prone to pass down
        from generation to generation

and even though we still stand   six feet   apart
in our distancing and forced isolation,
    on the brink of this dark oblivion,
        we survive...
        ...together

    we heal...
    ...together...
        ...as one

So, this is what it takes

This spoken-word-poem was inspired by the condition of our times before, and now during, COVID-19.

We have come together as a race, despite skin colour, caste, creed or origin because now we have a common enemy.
It was originally written as a rant and some parts still read as a rant, but it evolved, as we, as human beings, came together united in our fear and grief, to fight against COVID-19, setting aside our differences.

How a Flock of Pigeons Got Me Through

Deborah Washington

The lockdown came as suddenly as a quick shove out a barroom door. One night I was making St. Paddy's Day plans with a Scotsman – right off the boat – and the next day everything was shuttered. I never saw the Scotsman again – or anyone else, for weeks.

In the initial phase of restrictions I was surprised by the anxiety I felt. I couldn't concentrate. Couldn't get that opus written down though I had all the time in the world… What was wrong with me?

For hours I sat glued to my phone and read everything in print. Tried to get my head around what was going on. I was drowning in news stories and needed a lifeline.

I turned to social media and offered my services to help others: shopping, deliveries, anything. Initially I was asked to help out here and there, but the local community network was so strong and well-organized, my unfamiliar name perhaps got lost in the shuffle. After a few weeks, I was no longer called.

By the third week of total lockdown I was pacing the floors of my bachelor apartment in the North End of the city. I needed something useful to do. At a time when we were all self-isolating at home, I was by myself and I craved connection beyond the Internet.

I found it in a flock of pigeons.

It was the end of March. The grey days and oppressive dampness weighed heavily on my spirits. There was nothing to do but go for a walk. That day I traipsed empty downtown streets, peered into darkened shop windows. Eventually I wandered down an alley that several restaurants backed on.

It was eerily silent and the trash that usually spilled over the bins was long gone. The only sign of life was a flock of scrawny black pigeons, huddled together on the freezing pavement. The businesses that normally provided sustenance for these birds, had been closed for weeks and the flock was threatened with starvation. It seemed they didn't know where else to go for food, so they remained in their back-alley deathbed, helplessly waiting for some hand to feed them.

The poor things were visibly weakened by hunger and cold. They didn't even bother to fly away when I approached. A few wretched creatures perched on clumps of sod that formed between the pavement and the wall, perhaps to insulate their feet from the punishing cold of the asphalt. It was a pitiful sight. And a few sad carcasses were strewn about. I gathered them up and wondered if the other pigeons knew they too were close to death.

That afternoon I returned with some wild birdseed from the feeders I kept at home. I scattered a few handfuls, expecting a feeding frenzy.

The pigeons barely mustered enough energy to peck. They were slow to register the food and slower still to consume it. The creatures holding up the wall didn't even react to the seed I set before them. I knew my arrival came too late for some birds and I left the lane, vowing to return each day with my sack of seed.

The next day I tallied two more carcasses. One leaned against the wall, exactly as he'd been the day before. This time, though, the rest of the flock gathered around me when I scattered the seed...and they started to eat.

I watched the birds feed. I noticed, with some repulsion, how unhealthy they looked. Dull greasy feathers, so thinned in some places that I could see the white skin of their scrawny pale necks beneath.

The following day I was relieved there were no new dead bodies. After a few more days I switched to sunflower seed because of the higher fat content. Soon I detected a bit more pep to their steps. They ate earnestly too, adroitly snapping up the shiny black seeds.

Every day I measured five cups of seed into a plastic bag and headed to the alley. I positioned myself on a concrete step – avoiding the white spots of guano – and watched the pigeons until the last morsel was located and consumed.

I read somewhere that pigeons are quite intelligent and can remember faces.

They must have recognized mine because the following days, when I rounded the corner – as if on signal – the whole flock flew toward me. They hovered above my head like an ominous black cloud then followed me into the alley. I felt like the Pope on his balcony in St. Peter's Square, addressing his admiring flock. I imagined I looked like the crazy bird lady from some horror movie. But I didn't care.

My mission worked. I had a daily goal. It involved a thirty-minute walk each way that became my constitutional. A flock of birds relied on me and I depended on their well-being to feel useful. And more importantly, at a very lonely time, this ritual gave me a connection to other living things.

Truly, we were all in it together. The effects of the pandemic had trickled down to affect even the gentle, yet often maligned pigeon…birds that share our city streets and public spaces all over the planet. They rely on us. Our habits affect their habits. Our plight becomes theirs.

As a newcomer to the city, I didn't know anyone. I missed out on the Zoom parties that people were having all over town. But I didn't mind. I had my flock.

The flock became my friends. I sat with them. I talked to them.

Coaxed them a little closer. Their funny bobbing heads made me laugh.

The pigeons eyed me with curious nonchalance and I eyed them with motherly concern. I was anxious but relaxed a little when my new wards gradually plumped up and regained energy. With that my anxiety relaxed a little.

Then one morning I got a pleasant surprise. I heard the first coos and trills of pigeon breeding. My pigeons were mating! It was then I knew they would make it. And I was going to make it too. Most of us would.

After seven faithful weeks of daily feeding, I vanished from their lives. We had made it through the worst – the pigeons and I – and it was time for me to leave town. The shops and restaurants backing onto the alley opened again. People were out and about. The normal, albeit altered, routine of living had resumed.

Sometimes I wonder if the flock looked for me in the days and weeks that followed my departure. I'm sure they did. And do. After all, I brought them food.
One day I'll go back to the city, to that alley, to my pigeons. I'll see their offspring and they won't recognize me. I'll thank my pigeons, maybe with outstretched arms and head thrown back. Crazy bird lady.

Bring the Silver

Jan Fancy Hull

The assurance that clouds have *silver linings has comforted our distresses for centuries. Like most aphorisms, this one is true often – but not always.*

Through this lockdown I have a supply of silver tucked away in a secret drawer, in a box at the back of a top shelf, and in my heart, ready to be brought out and stitched into a persistent low-hanging cloud.

For me, poetry often brings the silver. We read poems carefully as we examine and internalize the message of each line. Focusing on the meaning or beauty of language distracts us momentarily from the misery du jour and brings a moment of respite, a silver lining in itself.

I often read these poems during lockdown. And through each, I'm not isolated, I'm solitary. These focused moments in a pandemic cannot be altered. Each one contains a brilliant concept larger than the scene that frames it: right and wrong; finding joy; courage – attributes the pandemic has called on us all to notice.

The Longest Day
Jan Fancy Hull

Summer solstice comes this afternoon.

The morning was cloudy and dull,
spring's parting gesture a cold shoulder.
By noon the sun has warmed the world.
Armed in dungarees, boots, gloves, bug spray,
I ineffectively wield yard and garden tools
in the perennial joust with weeds.

The work smells so good.
I swing into the saddle of my trusty lawn tractor
to cut the over-achieving grass before tomorrow's
rain.
I beg pardon of each and every bee that tugs on
white clover as I lift the whirling blades high over
them.

There are so many ways to do wrong, so few right.

I want oranges and bacon for tomorrow's brunch.
On my cross-country drive to the store, I see
rainbows in the ditches and fields:

yellow and green and white and purple blossoms.
My confession: I don't know their names
other than clover and buttercups and daisies,
and dandelions. And dandelions.
I am content in my botanical ignorance.
I don't need their names to see their beauty.

I'm certain they don't know mine.

I return with groceries and a distilled beverage
with a strong perfume of juniper.
The lake, at the verge of my green lawn,
reflects a sky I cannot describe,
in a mirrored depth I cannot fathom.
I sit by the lake and tune in to nature's
opera starring robin redbreast who appears
without fail at this festival every summer.
I watch the pair of loons diving and surfacing,
watch the tiny and indescribably blue fly, watch
heavy clouds begin to rumble in.
I remember that this is the hour summer arrives.

I am aware of it, though I do not know its name.

I Left the Earth

Jan Fancy Hull

I left the earth
for a while today. I was beneath a
tree with crayon-yellow leaves. I would
show you a photo but you would say, "Nice picture.
Wow!" It was so much more than wow. And above the
leaves, the sky, oh, the sky today. Blue is such a dull tool to
describe all the joy in that life-sustaining realm above us.
So I ascended. I brushed aside the leaves, moved past
the branches, into that sky. Don't worry, I didn't go
very high. I still felt the warmth of this autumn sun on my
back, heard the lake lapping against the shore, its
glass surface pushed into ripples by the light breeze.
When I looked down, I was
in my chair
again, my
book in
my lap.
I hadn't
fallen.
But for a few
moments, I did rise

Flags

Jan Fancy Hull

Morning air warms slowly, but it cannot reach
the frost already stored in the ironstone boulder
I rest upon.

Tall grasses waved green around this stone in summer.
Now, rigid and sepia-toned, each blade
is a faded photograph of its younger self.

But dry grasses still have much to do.
When the hard storms come, grass will stand and fight them all,
weapons high, stiff but weakening under cold hard rain.
Winds will whine like sirens through these blades. Ice pellets will
beat their snare-drums as they strike these dried flags of the resistance,
thrumming the approaching winter's march.

Was any rebellion against oppression fought more bravely?
Each one alone, courageous, these grasses remain upright,
on guard for the next assault. But they will not survive the onslaught.
Snow will fall, snow on snow, snow on snow.

We fight so fiercely to live, hoping to choose how and when we die.

Snow melts. In spring, new grasses rise up.
The old is dead, is thatch, is past.

I want to linger beside this brave grass and bear witness to its battles,
hear its patriotic songs, watch it parry the blows,
sit by its side in its final hours, show it some love.
But my boulder-seat is hard and cold as iron,
and I have battles of my own to wage while I am still able.

Stiffly, I rise.

THE BLUE DRESS
Heather D. Veinotte

During this time of the COVID-19 pandemic, I've been thinking about relationships and how the little things we do for friends and family may not seem like a lot to us, but have a huge positive impact on those we love and how we remember them, what we feel at peace with and what we regret. Not everyone could be with their loved ones who died during the COVID pandemic. And maybe some people dwell on that, rather than the fond memories that would bring them comfort.

Diane took Aunt Marion's hand and leaned over the hospital bed and kissed her wrinkled cheek. Tissue-thin eyelids fluttered open and when she saw Diane's face, she sighed.

"I'm so glad you're here," she whispered.

Diane blinked away the tears gathering at the corners of her eyes. "I can't think of anywhere I'd rather be."

A nurse entered the room and checked the beeping monitor on the other side of the bed. She touched Marion's arm.

"Diane's visits always make you happy."

Marion wet her lips and whispered, "I love her visits."

The nurse checked the chart at the foot of the bed and shook her head sadly at Diane. "I know you do, sweetie."

She leaned over Marion. "When the pain returns, I want you to ring the bell right away. Promise?"

Marion sighed. "I promise."

"Now, I'm going to let the two of you visit." She leaned over to Diane.

"When she becomes restless, call me and I'll ease the pain."

Diane nodded as she left.

"Tomorrow's your birthday, Aunty."

"I know dear. Ninety-seven. I find that so hard to believe."

Diane smiled and touched her aunt's hand. "Amazing, isn't it?"

Marion took a deep breath. "One always hopes you make a difference on this earth with the time you've been given. I hope I made a difference in my ninety- seven years."

Diane took her aunt's hand and squeezed it.

"You've always made my life so much better."

"When, dear?"

"Oh, so many, many times, but one time I'll never forget was when Mom passed away."

Marion nodded, "That was such an awful time."

"You were there for me then."

"I was?"

Diane nodded, smiling. "Yes, you were."

She took a glass with a bobbing straw from the tray and placed it to her aunt's dry lips.

"Have some juice."

Marion sucked on the straw and drank deeply, nodding to Diane to remove it. "I always seem to be so thirsty."

"I know, honey. It's the drugs."

"What did I do for you, dear? I can't seem to remember."

Diane smiled. "I can remember as if it was yesterday."

Marion whispered, "You'll have to tell me. I've forgotten."

"Well, it was the last week in June. Just a few days from the end of the school year. Mom had passed away the month before and Dad and I went to live with Grampy and Aunt Florence."

"I remember that. Such an awful time for all of us."

"I was sitting in Grampy's metal hammock on the veranda, pushing it back and forth with my legs and feeling confused and lost. All the girls were talking that day in class about what they were going to wear on Grading Day. Do you remember, how in Grade Four and up, the classes would march from the Elementary School over to the High School and walk across the stage to receive their report cards from the principal?"

Marion nodded. "I remember when I had to do it. I was always so nervous about going on the stage."

Diane nodded. "Shortly after Mom died, friends and family came and packed everything in boxes and moved our entire house to the barn and garage at Grampy's. We took our personal boxes to his house, but there were lots of containers that had to be unpacked and some of my boxes were still in the garage by grading time. We couldn't find the box with my dresses. And we found my records, but not my record player.

"When I look back, I see it must have been so hard on Dad. I must have been a horrible handful, being rooted from my home and dealing with the loss of Mom. Aunt Florence was lovely, and I loved her so much, but she really didn't understand how important it was for me to blend in, especially at that time. She said that I could wear one of her dresses."

Marion smiled. "Oh dear."

"That's why I was thrilled when you arrived in the driveway. I thought you could help me look for the box with my dresses. I did not want to wear a dress that my forty-year-old aunt wore. That was an old woman's dress. Unfortunately, I told her that."

They both started chuckling.

"Oh, poor Florence. She didn't quite understand about clothes and young girls."

"And to make matters worse, I had to deal with Linda Purcell, the class bully who was also the mayor's daughter. We all knew that because she would announce it at least five times a day. She was a nasty piece of goods and after Mom died, I became her target."

"Oh my. The apple doesn't fall far from the tree. I went to school with her mother and she was the class bully as well. Only her father owned the lumber mill. Her name was…Ernestine."

"Gosh, no wonder she was a bully, with a name like Ernestine."

Marion's chuckle changed to fits of coughing.

Diane took the glass and offered her some more juice. Marion drank deeply. Tiny beads of sweat glistened on her forehead.

Diane took her aunt's hands. "How's the pain?"

"It's…not…bad."

Diane snorted, "You lie."

"Yes dear, and right now…badly."

On the table close to the bed, a moist cloth lay folded on a tray of ice. Diane took it and wiped her aunt's face.

"Oh, thank you." She paused for breath. "That feels so nice and cool."

Marion's eyes closed. Her shallow breathing blended in with the beeping and humming of the monitors. Diane took her right hand and held it gently. The skin was so thin and fragile.

Marion's left hand lay open on the cover of the bed. Diane watched as her aunt began pulling her hand into a fist and releasing it. Diane sighed and pressed the CALL button.

The nurse had come and gone. Marion's hands finally relaxed against the covers. Later, her eyelids fluttered open. She smiled. "You're still here."

"You bet, where else would I be? I have delicious apple juice with ice, imported all the way from the fridge. Would you like some?"

"Oh yes, please." Marion took a deep drink and sighed. "I think about your mother a lot."

"Oh, so do I." After Mom died, it gave me so much comfort to have you close to me. You looked so much like her."

"Well, after all dear, we are identical twins."

"I know, even Grampy had a hard time telling you apart."

"I wish I could remember more about that time. Did I help you find a dress?"

"Yes, we searched all afternoon and finally found the box with my dresses."

Marion smiled, puzzled. "And that meant so much to you?"

Diane grinned and shook her finger in her aunt's direction. "Be patient, there's more to the story."

She took the glass of juice and placed the straw between Marion's lips. Her aunt drank deeply.

"Oh my. That's lovely."

"So," Diane said as she touched her aunt's cheek, "you stayed for supper and told me that you would pick me up the next morning and take me to school."

Marion's face beaded with sweat from the pain. Diane wiped her face with the cooled facecloth.

Her aunt whispered. "And did I?"

"Of course. You always did what you promised…. Okay, now I'm coming to the best part."

Marion smiled. "Finally."

Diane squeezed her hand. "Don't get saucy, lady."

"Well, the next morning you entered the kitchen carrying a huge white box tied with a blue bow and you laid it on the table."

"Why can't I remember?"

"You don't need to. I'm telling you what happened."

"When I raised the cover, layers of tissue exploded from the box. Underneath the clouds of tissue, was a dress. A beautiful, pale blue, Cinderella dress, with layers of frothy netting pushing out from underneath a chiffon skirt. The top layer of the skirt was pulled up into swags on the front of the dress and trimmed with white lace. The swags were held in place with blue fabric roses. The bodice of the dress was white lace and the blue chiffon puffed sleeves were trimmed with lace that matched the bodice. Wide blue chiffon ribbons attached at the waist and tied into a large fluffy bow in the back. Underneath the dress was a hairband with blue roses that matched the roses on my dress. It looked just like the coronet that

Cinderella wore in the movie. It was the most amazing dress I had ever seen. I stood in the middle of the kitchen floor and cried with joy."

Marion sighed as Diane removed the straw from her lips.. "I'm so glad it made you happy."

"It really did. So, you drove me to school. We laughed because I could hardly get in the car, my dress was so full. Aunt Florence had to push the skirts in before the car door could be closed.

"I walked into the classroom wearing my beautiful blue dress and my coronet of roses, feeling like a princess. Linda Purcell took one look at me and gasped. She just stared at me, speechless. I can tell you we all enjoyed the speechless part. I felt so wonderful. We were all so into Cinderella at that time. The girls kept telling me that my dress was exactly like the one that Cinderella's fairy godmother gave her for the ball."

Marion whispered. "I don't know about the fairy part, but I am your godmother."

Diane squeezed her aunt's hand.

"That day, you were my fairy godmother, too."

Diane caught the movement as her aunt's hand clenched the covers. She pressed the button for the nurse and cooled her aunt's face again with the cloth.

"Do you know, I still have that dress?" She placed the cloth back on the tray.

"What? *Nooooo!*"

"I do. When we were married, my flower girl wore it."

"That was the dress?"

"It was. And now it's packed away in my cedar chest and every time I see the white box, I remember how you made such a

horrendous time in my life so much better with your amazing kindness."

Marion whispered, "I did it because I love you."

Diane leaned over and kissed her aunt's cheek. "And I love you. Thank-you for always being there for me."

The nurse entered, moved to the monitors, checked the screens, her face full of compassion. She pulled the curtain around the entire bed and left Diane alone with her aunt.

As the beeping of Marion's life support machines slowed down and stilled, Diane wept as she held Marion's stilled hand against her own beating heart. So thankful and blessed for all the wonderful memories that had been created by this amazing woman and would forever be a part of her life.

INTERMENT DURING A TIME OF PANDEMIC
Bonnie L. Baird

We stand in this moment. In this enclosed circular columbarium. In the glow of countless oak niches. And natural light pouring about us from a skylight far above.

A wife of 70 years, a daughter, a son, a brother. And me, bearer of the ritual words. Each of us gowned in our thoughts. Maintaining our distance.

It's not a time for telling stories. That will come later. It's a time of pausing on the threshold of what lies beyond. All that space in such a little room.

I speak the old words that countless others before me have uttered: Earth to earth, ashes to ashes, dust to dust. So much unseen but felt is distilling into these moments. Floating about us.

The wife places the urn (heavier and more awkward than expected) into its niche. The distance between us, even in transference, maintains like a ritual dance. She steps forward, I step back. Together we say the last "amen."

I remember not to hug or shake hands as I promise to check in with them later, then step out to give them space to say goodbye.

After a time, the door clicks shut and it is still. Dust motes hang in the air, caught in the light streaming down.

Sometimes It's Too Much

Dylan B. Fassbender

Part I:

Sometimes it feels like too much. In some really intense moments it becomes overwhelming – a huge emotional release surrounded by darkness, conflict, drama, fighting, failure, pain. At the time, these outbursts feel normal to me, then later when the dust settles I can see things calmly. I try to use them as catalysts for reflection. As I reflect, I analyze and I can begin to piece together the puzzle of my emotionally driven words and behaviours. Only then can I compare non-emotional words and behaviors I might have used instead.

I have a mental illness that manifests as anger, depression, and a general malaise – the feeling that I am destroyed as a human being, as a person, physically, emotionally, and mentally. It's not the kind of "destroyed" that leaves a huge crater in the surface of the Earth. From inside I cannot gaze upon my human failure the way you can look down at the earth from a helicopter or airplane, and drift past the crater, seeing a simple, defined area of "wiped-out" terrain.

If only it were that simple, to erase then change a person's life, past, brain, heart, soul, moral code, purpose…. From my vantage point, just the thought of who and what I am gives me waves of anxiety. But now I am working to accept my reality, and try harder to communicate with those closest to me – the ones who decided to stay with me during this painful and unpredictable ride…. The ones who decided to keep me around….

Those caring ones allowed me to survive, rest, heal, and even to fall, and fall and fall yet again. And they bear witness as I cried and cried and cry now and they'll allow it when I'll cry in the future….

PART II: Before COVID-19

Wake up.
Anxiety seethes through my chest,
my heart pounds with a terrified thwack,
like it's trying to break out of my ribcage
to abandon me.

Some days I scream as I wake up
shake and whimper in the sheets,
"Don't make me get up,
not to this life,
not in this nightmare reality."
So I take another dose of whatever works,
and go back to sleep.
Sleep. Sleep. Sleep.

Sleep is the welcome time away from my life,
unless the nightmares get too horrific,
which they often do.

Then it's – Stay awake. Stay awake….
Stay Awake!
Any TV shows, movies and documentaries
keep my fickle mind occupied and awake.

Trapped inside,
in my dark, hopeless, loser apartment
in my parent's basement
I try to accept my shame, guilt, regret, and self-hatred.
I peek through the blinds to see how "bright" it is outside,
what time of day it is.

Otherwise, the blinds stay closed –
the darker the better,
and God forbid if anyone comes around the house and sees me.

What they must say about me….

Some have told me,
cruelly,
face to face.

They're right,
I am such a fucking loser.
A failure.
A drug addict.
A wanna-be, used-to-be, has-been, douche-bag artist.

I don't blame them for avoiding me.

I avoid myself more than they ever could

but the in-my-head voices
of the town's people out on those streets
shames me into isolation once again.
I don't go out
because people and problems with history wait there.
I can't go to the gym,
can't play sports,
can't walk the dog in the daytime,
can't go to the grocery store.

Just to the pharmacy and home.
As quickly as I can
and the pharmacy closes early.

I plan to go there late
because in the mornings
the wait can take hours.

On the bad days of withdrawal
I have scant minutes
between waves of cold sweats and shakes,
along with vomiting and shitting myself.

Vomiting and shitting yourself,
in case you haven't tried it,
is really shitty when you have to go into a pharmacy
where your high-school ex-girlfriend is the assistant manager
and the lights are so bright they melt you.

When I make it home safe
I return to my basement lair,

where I sit
fat
and drink myself to death.

My greatest question:
Do all nightmares have an end...?

Part III:

I truly search for roses among thorns – I look for the positive in every situation. I repeat and try to believe the mantra: You learn more from a loss than you do from a win – and I tell myself "Dylan, you should be learning from wins and losses." But it's hard to believe there's anything good to learn some days when everything seems like a loss.

And for my lost life, my losings, I try to believe that losing, will make me humble – a better person – or I'll become more kind and empathetic.

Another part of me places me in a different reality, tells me all these thoughts and unanswered questions will make me crazy.... They see-saw back and forth and I rise and sink in a rhythm that controls me.

Part IV:

It took me six or seven years to get this far down my dark, slow-motion, shit-life, of isolation in my hellish reality...and with the

COVID-19 pandemic lockdown, and the fear it causes, the rest of the world suddenly experiences some of what I experience every day with my mental illness. They're slowed down to my speed. They're afraid too. The world is forced to glimpse and deal with the fear I face each and every day.

Like me, no one goes outside during the COVID-19 lockdown and if they do it's only for essential things like I do.

And people lost their jobs and income or had to work from home instead of going to the office. They feared what they could not see – like I do.

People have it tough because of shutdowns and they tap into subsidies and seek help from many levels of government like I do. Some find relief; for others it is not so easy. Like me, they're trying to find their way back to normal.

In the blink of an eye people had no more leisure time with friends, no more walks outside in the sunshine, no more visits with family members. "Normal" people were experiencing what I do daily as I live and survive with my mental illness.

Others are forced to understand and crave what they can't and don't have – like me – even if they don't connect to me or others with mental illness. Maybe the world will be more welcoming and supportive after COVID-19. Maybe people will learn more from this than how to create a vaccine. More about compassion and walking a mile in another's shoes….

New Growth (Spring 2020)

Janet Barkhouse

Zoom, FaceTime, Skype threaten to forever
replace touch. Facebook, Instagram,
Twitter, like old radio shows, live to air,
crackle with horror. Hope trembles,
a fawn waiting for a doe hunted
and killed in Portapique. White, I kneel,
hands pocketed, on George Floyd's neck,
smash into Chantel Moore's home and shoot
and shoot and shoot and shoot and shoot.
What is it to be human? How to keep breathing?

I begin to garden. I weed the asparagus, the garlic,
damage a knee, weed the haskap bushes, plant
annuals. Weed the tomatoes, the herb garden, damage
an elbow, weed the annuals. I begin to remember

here not blood but maple blossoms stain the road
crimson. Waterlily shoots stretch awake
underwater, liminal. Each day another promise.

Tiny rhubarb heads crown earth, push cranberry red
through papery cowls, wrinkled leaves like alien hands
reach for light. Hummingbirds return. I remember

last fall: my cousins and I, clumsy in flotation suits,
our chartered zodiac swashbuckling to Isle Haute,
astonished to see in a world blue-grey a red spark
to starboard. A ruby-throated hummingbird, alone,
mid-sea, wind and waves rough post-Dorian.
It passes us, heading to Mexico. I begin to weed

my mind, examine old thoughts, roots entrenched,
twisted, intertwined. Isolation offers time to read:
The Tradition, Land to Light On, Blank.
Split Tooth, Legacy, Disintegrate/Dissociate.
White Fragility.

Each day thank Earth, its red sparks,
brave greens. Remember always I garden in Mi'kma'ki.
Take responsibility for unearned privilege, each day
give back. Remember Earth makes new life, made us.
Made us able to grow.

CHASING GLIMMERS

Bonnie L. Baird

My cat chases glimmers. He's a young cat, very active most of the time he's not sleeping.
He will spring up from wherever he's perched and just gaze steadily at one spot on the rug, on the wall, on the sofa or the TV or the floor. Stare without blinking, then hunch down, coil his muscles, or draw himself up on two legs, and...pounce!

Most of the time I can't see what he's chasing. But sometimes I do. It hovers, like I imagine Tinker Bell did, just there, just out of reach. If he does capture it, it flits over his paws and away.

He's climbed great heights in pursuit of it. With or without the aid of cupboards or bookcases. Stretched out full length and then some, reaching, reaching. *Where did it go?*

He's been on high alert by my side when I'm stretched out in bed late at night reading. I imagine him thinking. *It's somewhere in these folds. I can hear it moving.* Close to the surface. If I stay really, really still....

Tonight I stand on a darkened balcony, answering a Facebook call to light a candle and hold vigil for two minutes.

The province is reeling from a shooting that, by this morning's media tally, has caused injuries and 22 deaths – not including the shooter (interesting exclusion). The RCMP are beginning the gruesome, painstaking work of investigating 16 or more crime sites.

In this time of COVID-19 and self-isolation, there can be no funerals and no traditional honour guard for the RCMP officer who died. Families cannot gather to hold one another or weep together. Or colleagues or friends. The old rituals that help us transition from one stage of life to another or navigate tragedies cannot be practiced. At least, not as they have been.

I stand here tonight looking out over a cityscape that's quieter and darker than normal. Thinking of the pain radiating out from little communities and broken hearts across a nation that's already exhausted.

How do we bear this, when the elasticity of soul is almost gone?

In the dark, I notice two candles on a balcony to the left of mine and a couple standing vigil. Now some more—just to my right, there—down below me, and there—below that.

And I think of my cat's unwavering conviction that there are always glimmers to be caught. Even if they aren't visible.

A Friend Request for Philippe Petit*
Chad Norman

A reason to reach out, I have many.

Among all that you shared after the towers
the one answer, "Why? There is no why!"

And me, then, saying, "How can there be no why?"
or even, "What! No why?" I guess I will learn
the answer by pressing a button
I use to share hope during this duration
caused by a virus with actual intentions,
keeping us from our dreams, from our families,
a button found among many buttons
set in some kind of order on the keyboard
now truly a daily immediate lifeline.

A need, if you will. Already hung over our lives,
connected to one side of the virus and the other
we can call beginning and ending,
a wire we are all kind of out on
holding our custom-made balancing poles,
eyes on what each of us dare look at

being at so many different heights, able
to form smiles under our masked faces.

Philippe, I wonder if you will accept my request?
I promise I have no intention to ask you why
about the predictions, when the virus will end.

I just want a new friend, no matter the bridge,
no matter the cathedral, no matter the artist,
someone I, being out here using my flat feet
to understand each step will be taken, made
successfully, without doubt, willing to wait
for the others in front of me who also dare
walk the belief we can be one with the wire.

Tightrope walker

Three Hearts + Four
Ruth Ann Adams

Almost twenty years ago, my family and I moved from Ontario to Nova Scotia. We were blessed to maintain old friendships while forming new ones. Recently some of these relationships have interconnected in amazing ways.

On March 16th, an Ontario friend, Donna, and I exchanged a number of texts about her son, Curtis, and his three friends on a hiking trip in Peru.... After President Martin Vizcarra declared a state of emergency, including border closures, the boys tried to reach the airport in Lima.

But returning home wasn't that easy....

Donna texted that when Curtis' group arrived at Cusco, they met three young men from Halifax. Thinking that was interesting, I texted my Nova Scotia friend, Kelly, and told her what was going on with the Ontario boys.

Kelly texted:

```
I wonder if
one of the boys
might be Jordan,
the son of my
friend Carla.
```

Jordan was also travelling with friends in Peru.

After more texts back and forth Kelly put the pieces of the puzzle together. Donna's son, Curtis, and his group had met up with Carla's son, Jordan, and his friends, on a street in Peru!

Curtis texted his mom that one of the boys wore a Blue Jays cap so he'd asked them if they were Canadian. They were, and the three boys and four boys joined to become seven young men, trying to reach home.

The distance from Cusco to Lima was far too great to travel before the borders closed. The boys drove rental cars from Cusco to Arequipa. On some parts of their journey there were no roads, only dirt.

When they reached Arequipa, the Ontario group spent the night in a hostel while the other boys stayed at a hotel. In the morning, after a state of emergency was declared, the Ontario boys joined the Nova Scotia group at the hotel. The larger group was apprehensive about leaving the hotel, even to get food, because of the heavy police presence on the streets. The staff were wonderful though and at one point the head of security even made a trip for them.

On the home front, many contacts were made with officials in Nova Scotia and Ontario, on behalf of the boys. One friend sent emails to provincial premiers every hour on the hour. Many people here, prayed for the boys' safe return.

On Facebook posts, the defining signature became three hearts plus four hearts, for the seven boys.

♡♡♡ + ♡ ♡ ♡♡

The Canadian government began sending in planes to bring back stranded Canadian citizens. Finally, the seven young men were taken by bus to Lima, and then from a military airport, they boarded a flight to Canada.

What were the chances that four young men from Ontario would meet the three from Nova Scotia on a street in Peru, that they would join up and travel together and then find out there was actually a connection between two groups, through my friends in both provinces?

Coincidence?

No. I believe the boys were brought together for mutual support and protection. My friend, Kelly, put the pieces of the puzzle together, which led to Carla, Donna and others building relationships of mutual support, comfort and finally, shared joy.

Until this call to action, Donna and Carla were complete strangers, living in two provinces. They were brought together at an appointed time, just as their sons were, for a common purpose: Get the boys home. I call this a divine appointment, though some will perhaps call it coincidence.

The story of Curtis, Jordan and his friends reminds us that we don't have to be alone and that working together can create happy endings.

No matter what happens in the days ahead, I will always associate COVID-19 with three hearts plus four hearts, a reminder of seven brave young men, and new friendships formed.

Hello!

Chad Norman

For those self-isolating along with me during the virus invasion, April 2020.

It has been said
over and over
"back to normal."

I stop and inquire,

"just when was that?"

Portals

Jennie McGuire

Portal: An entrance, a gateway, a threshold.
But the word also conjures up a crossing-over, a new awareness, the quest for the unknown, a deeper understanding of the self.

Our lives are a series of Portals which we pass through whether we are ready or not.

The power we have is the choice to hang on, or to let go of the things buoying us up, or weighing us down.

Passing through a Portal is ultimately a courageous act.

JENNIE MCGUIRE

This collection of "Portals" is all mixed media - watercolour, acrylic, ink and collage.

Portal Image 1   Jennie McGuire

Portal Image 2   Jennie McGuire

Portal Image 3   Jennie McGuire

Portal Image 4   Jennie McGuire

RUSTWORKS
Beverley McInnes

As a juried Craft Nova Scotia member and multi-media artist working in rust, metal and found objects, Beverley McInnes finds creating her art rewarding as each piece allows for growth and discovery. Living in Chester, NS Beverley ferrets out and finds inspiration from the decay, found objects and discarded rust for her installations. Her RUSTWORKS are then transformed into large pieces for a garden or outdoor setting while smaller ones may be displayed.

Beverley is fascinated by her shadow, uses it in many different ways, elongating it and playing with the image. She translates into her work so much of what she has experienced throughout her life and during this COVID-19 time.

She collages with rust, rock and stone, image transfers, copper and brass to enhance whatever found objects dictate with their inherent shape. The completed piece is then mounted.

"My RUSTWORKS speak to me about seeing something beautiful in the discarded, giving new life to what has been broken and cast out and seeing worth in what has been deemed worthless. There is value in the valueless...."

BEVERLEY MCINNES
Multi-media, Assemblage, Collage, Rust, Metals & Found Objects

Rustworks 1   Beverley McInnes

Rustworks 2   Beverley McInnes

Rustworks 3   Beverley McInnes

We've Got This

Glenda Pennell & Melanie Donnelly

You can hear the song - and sing along at
https://youtu.be/QCgMUMjsJzc (Glenda) or
https://www.youtube.com/watch?v=r9vAjUCaj4c (Melanie).

Glenda Joy Pennell and Melanie Donnelly wrote "We've Got This" during the 2020 COVID-19 pandemic to offer strength and hope by highlighting togetherness and some of the positive outcomes experienced during the quarantine.

Lyrics, melodies, rhythms and arrangement were composed via email, Messenger, texts/telephone calls and Zoom to maintain social distancing. Neither artist had worked in this way before and they are delighted with the song they wrote together. Their hope is that "We've Got This" brings a little joy to Gathering In *readers as well.*

We've Got This

Glenda Pennell & Melanie Donnelly – © August 2020

Did you ever think that the world could become so unfamiliar?
An invisible foe would cause a lockdown
Isolated and stuck at home in our private bubbles
6' apart in a mask and gloves when we have to go to town

Do you believe that in every cloud there is a silver lining?
That darkness breeds appreciation for the coming light
And that absence truly makes the heart grow fonder
If you focus on the wonderment you might

PRE-CHORUS:
Hold on, we're all in this together
The whole wide world is finally at one

CHORUS:
This is not the 1st hardship we've had to endure
We've been here before
And we've got this
Don't worry we've got this
God knows we've got this

Do you see all the clever ways we've found to stay connected?
How we're learning that when united we're stronger
And Mother Nature is showing signs of rejuvenation
Thanks to quiet roads less travelled shore to shore

PRE-CHORUS:
Hold on, we're all in this together
The whole wide world is finally at one

CHORUS:
This is not the 1st hardship we've had to endure
We've been here before
And we've got this
Don't worry we've got this…ooohhh

BRIDGE:
What if this new normal makes us grateful
For what we took for granted before
Sharing all this precious time together
Enjoying our loved ones more

CHORUS:
This is not the 1st hardship we've had to endure
We've been here before
And we've got this
Don't worry we've got this
God knows we've got this
We've got this

THE CARNIVAL

Kathy France

Kathy France shares this link so you can listen to and read along as she performs this spoken-word Poem:
https://youtu.be/p7HUM9rQ8fk

A Carnival rolled into town one night
while I was sleeping.
Each morning it draws me in,
weeping, –
right into the horror of it….

It's the Contagion Carnival!
Listen,
the carnie calls:
"Step right up ladies and gents!
Try your luck!
Scrub, sanitize, purge, a surge of anxiety
Yours for a buck!
Step right up, but not too near.
Watch, read, listen.
Media overload all in a panic
feeling manic –
the fun fair of fear!"

A Carnival rolled into town one night
while I was sleeping.
Each morning it draws me in,
weeping,
with strange new rides called
social distancing
self-isolating
panic buying.
In the Haunted House
masked doctors pace corridors
packed with patients, dying.

Listen
The carnie calls:
"You sir, feeling lucky?
Test your strength against the plague!
How about you, ma'am?
Care to play this game of chance?
All right then!
Spin down the aisles in the Costco Dance!
Ride bumper-to-bumper cars on the holiday weekend!
But first, nip into Starbucks for a cotton candy latte!"

The sideshow freak show of counting the infected,
tallying the dead,
while the merry-go-round goes round
spinning dread.

The world now small.
Cities fall to an invisible enemy.
Economies stall

I ride the roller coaster of anxiety:
Afraid to go out
to engage
to converse
to breathe
Cross the street to avoid the stranger.
Back away from a dear friend –
 every surface: danger!

Gone are hugs
heads bent together in whispered conversations,
kisses on the cheek, loving-up the neighbour's cats

Here now…
unemployment, fines and KEEP OUT signs;
Flattening the curve;
Battening down the hatches;
toilet paper, hand sanitizer, bleach.

Like the wrong end of a grotesque whack-a-mole
I am hit again and again.

Did she just cough?
Will he move to the left or right?
How do I make a mask?
Can we survive this financially?
Why aren't Doritos listed as an essential food group?

This crazy Corona tilt ride has winded me.
I want off!
Come on fortune teller,
give us some good news.

And not just a vaccine.
I'm talking about an end
to the 1%
the billionaires
to profit margins and multi-nationals
to science deniers
to invasive bucket-list tourism
other skin colours, a means to an end
politics pandering to ignorance
rampant racism
idolatry of individualism
uncurbed consumerism
unchecked capitalism…
That's the disease that has been infecting this world for decades –
this planetary plague
this poison of our own making
while you were sleeping.

Breathe

Actions for now….
It is an act of hope
to really deeply notice a tree.
It is an act of love to call out to the neighbour you rarely see,
"How you doing?
Everything okay?"

Daily walks in the fresh air.
Gratitude for the Quiet
The Pause
The Small…

For spring flowers,
Zoom family meet-ups
and creatives on the Internet sharing their power.
This is all we've got right now.

When it's time, what will we go back to?
What will we carry forward?
What will we change?

I have an idea:
Let's unleash a pandemic of compassion.
Let concern for our shared planet go viral.

I see you and you see me:
Hearts as big as the world.

A Carnival rolled into town last night,
while we were sleeping,
its hard lessons worth keeping.

Teachings of Henny Penny

Alnoor Rajan Talwar

pieces of my heart
      shatter
    and fall
        like imperfections
            discarded...
...reminding me of Henny Penny's incessant natter
              of imminent disaster

Only, it isn't the sky that's falling
            It is Life, as I know it, and my heart breaking
    for it
And, as bits and pieces
      break and float,
      loose and untethered,
          humanity is left
          seeing red,
          miffed,
    accidentally, forcibly and unprecedently

      united
in its anger and grief
  at this,
     another predicament

I was reading a book on cherished children's stories and I re-read "The Story of Chicken Little," and how panic led the animals to a worse fate. In our case, our choices can lead us to a worse fate. Most people follow the precautionary advice. Many don't.

For now, we're united in our fear, anger and grief.

THE FASCINATING "TRAUMA" OF BEING QUARANTINED!

Dorothy Grant

COVID-19 happened not long after we made a significant change in our lives. You see, a few years ago when my husband Bill and I had reached our 80s, we decided to sell our home and move to a seniors residence in the South End of Halifax that would provide us with a much more appropriate environment.

Candidly, I can tell you our lives since then have been pleasant but, certainly not "exciting." Our situation and atmosphere certainly changed dramatically, when, in early spring, we learned that COVID-19 (the Coronavirus disease) – believed to have originated in China – was ruthlessly killing countless people around the world.

At first, we tended to rationalize our situation a little and tried to convince ourselves that Nova Scotia, hopefully, would avoid such a frightening disaster.

Unfortunately, that was naive thinking because we soon had to face the distressing reality that the virus's insidious dimensions had invaded Nova Scotia and as a result, more than fifty seniors living in Northwood Manor in Halifax along with others had died of it in Nova Scotia.

Almost immediately we were informed by our residence management that we all would face and deal with major transitions if they were to ensure our health and safety during this pandemic. We would no longer enjoy eating our meals in our residence's very attractive dining room. This meant for this time, we wouldn't share engaging conversations with many of the very interesting residents that had often dined with us.

Instead, our meals were delivered to our rooms on trays, by staff members dressed in knee-length yellow garments that practically covered their bodies.

In addition to this attire, they wore face masks and their hands were covered by protective plastic gloves.

I have to admit that I smiled a little at their presentation because it reminded me of my first position as a graduate nurse at the IWK Hospital for Children when I prepared myself to assist in the operating room!

But as time passed and the pandemic swept through the region we learned more about the unwelcome effects the contagious COVID-19 would have on us.

We were notified that weekly musical performances and lectures about subjects associated with our relevant health issues were cancelled, as well as the monthly event to celebrate residents' birthdays.

We complied with the new rules, however there was one thing that was really difficult for us to accept. Most visits to our apartments were "outlawed."

In our case, this meant our son Ian, who is a doctor at the Halifax Infirmary, was no longer allowed to meet with us! Honestly, with that lockdown we suddenly felt so alone, deprived of his essential good counsel and his medical wisdom.

At the time, I found myself thinking of other residents who lived there in our residence. Particularly on my mind, were those who were alone there, seniors who had truly thrived because of the visits they received from close relatives and good friends.

I admit that on occasion, I felt somewhat isolated too but when that happened, I recognized what was happening and quickly did some "soul searching." In this way I began spending my "down time" consciously contemplating cherished memories. I created a list and added to it when things came to mind.

This recap enabled me to focus more on recall of rewarding "episodes" and particularly moving experiences that contained highlights of our lives together.

As the weeks went by, the list grew. It drew thoughts of our very happy marriage, and of our two sons – sadly, that included memories of our beloved son David who had been a real joy until the age of eleven when he died of a fatal neurological condition at the IWK Hospital for Children.

The memory of David is forever etched on our hearts.

For me, isolation was all about being "elsewhere" somehow, and another fascinating diversion for me was to reflect on the satisfaction I had found during the many years I was a consumer reporter with the Canadian Broadcasting Corporation in Halifax.

During that time, I worked closely with many individuals to help them deal with outrageous exploitations and to help others address and overcome unfair scenarios in their lives.

I also chose to vividly recall situations where I had encountered abject poverty and where people barely existed on a sparse lifestyle. This process taught me to value the intangible things that many of us take completely for granted! I found that recognizing these times and feeling gratitude for little things shifted my moods and thoughts in a more positive direction.

During one of my contemplations I recalled an article where I researched and wrote about the 1918 Spanish flu pandemic that – long before COVID-19 – had similarly terrorized the whole earth.

At the time, Halifax and Dartmouth were rebuilding after the deadly Halifax explosion that claimed nearly 2000 lives and devastated their North End communities.

Of course, at the time, no one would have believed a terrible flu would soon kill more Nova Scotians than had died during the Halifax Explosion the previous year!

As the Spanish flu ruthlessly spread its vicious agenda, newspapers in Halifax published daily reports, listing new cases, infected occupants' addresses…and sadly, many deaths. Sound familiar?

To handle the numbers succumbing to the flu, Dartmouth and Halifax opened hospital beds at the quarantine facility on Lawlor

Island; reopened the unused wards in the Victoria General Hospital; and built a new facility in Willow Park.

Men began wearing face masks and health authorities from Halifax dealt with the massive numbers of deaths by ordering all bodies buried immediately, without church services.

A Halifax man I interviewed recalled being told, "They threw them in a hole just like animals."

It was not uncommon that people lost several members of their immediate families, and the community was shaken with anxiety, fear and hard times.

Halifax's and Dartmouth's Boards of Health took other initiatives to stop the flu from spreading. They ordered all public gathering places – including churches, theatres, schools, and restaurants – to reduce their open hours, or close completely.

It is important to point out that television didn't exist at that time, to provide hourly guidance as is the case now. And there wasn't any kind of government monetary assistance when jobs were lost or income streams dried up. In those days households had one provider.

Food banks hadn't been created and families were larger, so hunger was a reality for many. It was a time when many people experienced hopelessness.

By the end of December 1919, almost 2,000 Nova Scotians had died from the pandemic, while at least another 281 died between January and April 1920 for a total of some 2,265 dead – more than the deaths in the 1917 Halifax Explosion.

You might wonder why I choose now to share the cruel temperament of a pandemic that took place over a hundred years ago....

Let me explain: I did this to underline the fact, that the human race has the awesome ability to survive horrendous manifestations such as the Spanish flu and COVID-19 and, mysteriously, it manages to find a secret place in our brains where memories of these awful demons will be locked away or conveniently forgotten as time passes.

Like it or not, that's exactly what happened before and one must predict it will happen again!

THIS TIME THE GOVERNMENT IS GOOD FOR YOU

Dr. Gregory V. Loewen

This time the government is good for you.

Relax with this advice, I'm a doctor. Of philosophy, that is. I hold a world top-40 Ph.D. in the human sciences and partly because of this people often ask me to "explain" what is going on right now. I can't cure the virus, so my skills are not front and centre. But step aside with me for a moment, and I'll attempt to tell you why I think that this time, the government is the right pill for the job.
Needless to say, as a thinker I am no great fan of the State. Our official apical ancestor, Socrates, was executed by the State for "corrupting youth," which remains a large part of my mission. Kant was ordered by his State to stop writing about religion, a particularly delicate theme in his time – even more than our own. He ignored the order and no doubt, in response, said something that wasn't fit to print. So that's pretty much where I come from in the day to day, when times are mundane and life seems long.

But for the moment, our times are neither. I recently published a new theory of anxiety and so one thing I can tell you right off is that Anxiety, capital "A," is seen by philosophers as a good thing.

It's like an early warning system, an impetus to care, which Heidegger stated was the most fundamental aspect of our beings. This "concernfulness," as he put it, orients ourselves to the most pressing of issues which underlie the day to day of living on. These include the condition of others to self, the future as "being ahead of ourselves," and our thrown and fallen state as beings who exist in the envelope of both "finitude" – existential finiteness that cannot be located at a precise time, just as we cannot know the hour of our individual deaths – and "running on" – moving toward our future deaths but in no conscious or systematic manner.

Large-scale crises are certainly something to work against and around, but they also serve to distract and decoy us away from confronting the intimacy of our own deaths, which cannot be shared with any other human being.

So ironically, part of our anxieties regarding COVID-19 concerns how well this crisis will distract us from ourselves, our own lives as we have lived them and whatever regrets we may have suppressed about them. Anxiety, on the other hand, alerts us to these more intimate aspects of selfhood and does not let us be distracted by the world in any inauthentic manner.

Generally, the State is part of this decoy world, issuing this or that decree that appears abstracted from our daily life, even arbitrary. The State is one of theological philosopher Paul Ricoeur's two examples of the "evil of evil" (the other being the Church). The evil of evil is defined as "fraudulency in the work of totalization." What does this mean?

Traditionally, only the gods were omniscient and omnipresent. As secular political life elbowed spiritual life into the margins, indeed, sometimes into the shadows, the State replaced the Church as the centre of social power. Even so, as a human institution, government is flawed, not at all all-knowing, and not quite everywhere at once. It often pretends that it is both, and in this it is a fraud. Many modern institutions partake in this "fraudulence" as they pretend to be everything for everyone.

The university is another obvious example. But with the stern demands the State places upon us these days it is flexing its absolute power over civil society, in part, again, and perhaps ironically, to keep it thus. We are reminded of Lord Acton's almost cliché epigram, originally in epistolary form, that "power corrupts," and further "absolute power corrupts absolutely." So we might be adding this worry to our list of anxieties and generally – and in principle – we should always be concerned about limiting the power of the State, lest more governments arise around the globe and lengthen the list of authoritarian regimes.

But this time I'm going to tell you that our governments, at least, are doing the right thing. Listening to real doctors, for instance, and following their advice to the letter. In turn, we as civil and unselfish citizens need to do the same.

This does not mean that we shed our individuality for automata, slough off our would-be immortal coils of freedom for slavery and obedience – we might often wish our freedom was unlimited in contrast to our actual lives – or regress to the status of young children. To take advice is a choice we make, one based on the best of our knowledge at the time, and one that the vast majority of us, myself certainly included, could not know and fathom all the subtleties to make an informed decision ourselves.

We do not become thoughtless morons by acceding to this common will. Indeed, it is thinking that has brought us to this point and it is thinking that will see us through to its far end, however indefinite this may appear to be today. At both federal and provincial levels then, we should heed to the letter the demands of the day. So relax, take two governments, and call me in the morning.

NOVA SCOTIA LOCKDOWN
Cynthia French

In his mural, *Dream of a Sunday Afternoon
in Alameda Central Park*, a young Diego holds hands
with the skeleton woman, La Catrina,
links arms with her creator Posada; this, the first
time she appears in Rivera's work; he appears
in front of Frida Kahlo as a boy, a boy
who holds hands with death. Frida
haunts every shop, street stall,
gallery and bar in Mexico, as does La Catrina –
every day The Day of the Dead.

At the centre of the dream scene
in her elegant bones, elaborate boa,
and plumed hat, Catrina stands with Diego
in this mural as she did all his life, her skull
grinning at the joke. Diego's twin brother died at one
and a half. Like all his brothers and sisters, Rivera carries death
in the arms of his life.

In Nova Scotia, it's been six weeks of sickness
and death, and a weekend beyond
the grave. Colchester County is home to Great Village,

where Elizabeth Bishop's *little moons fall down like tears*
from the almanac hanging above the Little Marvel Stove. Sorrow
upon sorrow. Our beloved poet wrote loss
as polished art. At my desk, La Catrina framed in sparkles
on a matchbox we bought in San Miguel.
Was it only March?

April snow and gray light, COVID-cold wind,
gunmetal lake. Bishop, Rivera, and Frida weave dark
and light, death and life, show us, the stricken
and weary, how to look, bear witness, listen – weep
into teacups. Numbed by tragedy we look, bear witness,
sing, play bagpipes, weep and grin.

Nova Scotia rising from numberless
days, positive counts, clotting lungs, elders
dying alone, to neighbours and families killed in hate.
We tie blue and gold tartan on a gate, light
a lone candle, pick one daffodil.

You've been a bird without wings in a house
without doors long enough,
says Rumi.

Compassion builds a door –
restlessness cuts a key.

The match flames in the room behind locked
doors. The daffodil dances, the ruffle of
her skirt freed at last from spring snow.

My skin itches all day. At night I dream feathers –
the mourning dove puffs her mauve breast,
nods and moans. Does she seek something
lost – *door keys, an hour badly spent?* Look,
look again at the light.

One lone beam, like brass in her beak.

Earth Day 2020

Barbara Menzies

A tiny, stealthy virus
turns the planet upside down!

Days grow longer…
Time, longer still…

Confined to our quarters
we emperors of the earth
long for the glory days
of liberty, touch and space,
free-range globe trotting

Open the windows!
Breathe the pure air!
Hear the spring chorus
of birdsong and frog voices,
a rising crescendo
on every continent!

Wild creatures roam empty runways,
reclaim silent city streets.
Who are the zookeepers now?

The human world on PAUSE
mourning our losses,
heavyhearted,
while the natural world
breathes deeply
and relishes the REFRESH.

OBLIVION'S WAKE
David Huebert

We danced naked in the living room. We sat in a plastic sled in the backyard, paddled the grass with twigs. We played tug of war with a towel. We raced through the basketball court, galloping contagions of joy. The toddler begged never to go back to daycare. We built forts on the couch. We invaded the bathroom when my spouse, Natasha, tried to sneak a shower. We cleaned the fridge, hung paintings, potted plants – the baby proudly munched soil. We froze homemade Popsicles, baked chocolate chip cookies, scarfed batter, licked spoons. The toddler wailed hysteric down the stairs.

Our dryer had broken, and sheets were splayed like sails over the couch – the toddler was sure her mother had built a fort without her in the night. Bath time got old. Dancing naked got old. The toddler begged to go back to daycare.

The toddler comes up the stairs, screaming, "Papa! Papa!" Her little sister has yanked her hair again. Cuddle break on the bed.

Pandemic or not, raising little kids is a battle of will, patience and creativity. A week of staycation had been fun for the children and good for the family. By week two, we parents were worn, drained, wracked for ideas. All city parks had been closed for a week, including the playground we can see from our living room window.

Before isolation, we never kept the kids home all day. Their daily rhythm involved at least two outings: dance class, pool, library, playground, soccer, Grandma's house, Point Pleasant Park. We are still working out the new routines, how we can snatch a minute, an hour…to rest, shower, write. The child-care era has been replaced by the epoch of asking whether this is a suitable time to sneak a bowel movement. Daily, hourly, we mine new forms of play.

My two children play "evil wolf" on the bed, gnawing at each other's tummies, coaxing; their mother herding, giggling, devouring.

There are shades of privilege in the bruise of my distress. As I write, Natasha wrangles the children, loads the dishwasher, wards off sugar and iPads. In our daily lives, we can (barely) afford childcare. We have a roof over our heads. We're not sick. Our children, thankfully, are not old enough to understand the dangers or to desperately miss their closest friends.

Natasha lost her work (and purpose) weeks after returning from maternity leave. I, like many other men, have leaned on my partner. At times she's leaned back.

Explosive poop incident, known in our home as a "cacastrophe." Impromptu midday bath.

It's raining, fierce. I put the toddler's rain pants on, deploy her tiny, useless rainbow umbrella and brave the belligerence of March. We travel a block and a half before she asks to turn around.

Stopped there in the pommelling rain, the toddler spots another little girl, about her age, standing in a bay window. I kneel down with my daughter, and wave. Waving into a stranger's house – something I would never have done before isolation. Something that might have embarrassed me, and that I would have discouraged in my children. But we stand in the beating rain. Stand and wave to this strange girl. My way of letting my daughter know that the world is out there, that other children are out there – in their windows. That they too are lonely, seeking connection, needing and making new forms of play.

Inconsolable meltdown: cause undetermined though clearly related to the plastic machinery of a make-at-home Popsicle kit.

Little children don't conform to adult logic – they bend it delightfully. They think that potty training has to do with locomotives, that the counterpart of penis should be "poonis." My children don't understand "disease," are satisfied with the vague notion that "everything is closed."

My children are oblivious, but, gratefully, they are also oblivions. They open seams in the flesh of the world, send me spilling through. It has been a joy, here in Pandemia, to swim the surf of their minds, to ride oblivion's wake.

Nap time.

Yes, the toddler asked to go back to daycare. But, more often, she asks to stay home forever. It turns out that our children's fundamental social need is simple: us. It's an acute exhaustion to be their only entertainers, but it's also enlivening and enlightening, a boot-camp of the ludic.

I'm grateful to have my vocation at my fingertips. And I am optimistic: Worldwide we are crafting, together, new ways of being social. Whatever the "return to normal" might look like, these new ways of playing will not be lost.

This essay was originally published as part of **CBC Books' Transmission Series.**

WITH LOVE...COMES HOPE
Alnoor Rajan Talwar

Nothing of any significance happened today
           The plants needed watering
      My body needed tending
Unlovely things were aplenty
So was beauty   I chose to ignore it

              I sit here...isolated and protected,
      my silence punctuated
          with the sounds of solitude

        An eternity lies between us
          and I hold on
             to Hope
        and the forever and ever of fairy tales,
        suffering the infinity
        in between

              Without you, I float...spiralling
                endlessly,
            with nowhere to fall

Yet, you're right here with me
        through each day and sufferance,
…in my every thought and frustrated utterance,
      in my prayers and pleas
      and in my innermost me,
           where I myself have yet to be

        Your brilliance
        makes me whole
When we are together,
     all complications fade
        and I wait with increased impatience,
           as day 65 comes…
                         …and goes
       I've spent
       one thousand, five hundred and sixty hours
         without holding you

At the end of each day,
I fall asleep…sinking into the ocean of dreams…
          with a tear and a smile
            …yearning and loving…

      …for with Love, comes Hope…

This poem was inspired by the people who were and are separated from loved ones due to COVID-19.
Hope and love are inherent human qualities that need to be cherished, valued and practiced.

BLESSINGS ON THE BROKEN ROAD
Chaya Gratto

I often say "Energy knows no bounds!" As a shamanic energy healer and medium, I was especially grateful that the restrictions placed on many workers during the COVID-19 crisis did not slow me down. For many of my clients, the connection to Spirit was an anchor in an ever-shifting landscape. I did not realize just how true that was until I met a client I'll call Andrea.

I did a first remote reading for Andrea, just before we headed into our COVID cocoons. What surfaced for me in our first session was that she was caring for her mother – in the final stages of cancer – and that she had a grown daughter heading down a dangerous path. She left the session feeling more emotionally supported than she had in a long time.

Three months later, I received an early morning message from her. I presumed that she was ready to book another session. But when I opened the message I learned her thirty-year-old daughter's body had just been found. Our conversation from March came flooding back to me and I heard "overdose." As Andrea started typing to me, I felt the telltale signs of spirit presence. I was awash with goosebumps – a connection was forming.

Andrea was still in shock; the uniformed police officers had just left her door. She was looking to understand and clearly, the young deceased woman had something to say to her mother. I gently asked if she was open to this. Her "Yes" – more like an exhale – was equal parts grief and relief.

I make it a point not to interfere with any messages given to me. I pass along what I receive, without allowing my ego to become involved. It's been a difficult promise to keep when I am shown or told things that I know will be hard for the heart to bear.

I steeled myself and told the client I saw that her daughter had passed in her apartment, alone. And from what I'd seen and felt, it looked like a drug overdose. In my mind's eye, her daughter's spirit walked through a grey, desolate landscape – my personal symbolism for depression.

Mom told me that her daughter had, in fact, battled mental illness and had not received the help she had needed. Texts found later on her daughter's phone confirmed that she had wanted to take her own life.

To validate it really was her coming through, the young woman showed me her well-defined calves from years of playing soccer and she let me know she was quite the pool shark, too! She also said she worried about her father and made reference to "the apple not falling far from the tree."

My client agreed and explained this remark by sharing that her daughter's father was an alcoholic. It was expected that he would take this news especially hard since he would carry his own guilt about the influence of his addiction, on top of his fresh grief.

Then I saw a striking image.... Her daughter stood on a beautiful stretch of coastline. She wore a short white dress and her arms, outstretched, reached toward the sky. I told her mother that she was expressing joy in her newfound freedom. Seagulls circled above her and she told me that she would send her Mom a sign that she was at peace – in fact, it would be in the form of a seagull. And I sensed the delivery of the gull would be more complex.

The client confirmed that her daughter had lived on the East Coast and together, they had made many memories that involved expanses of rocky shoreline with gulls overhead. However, the mother now lived in a land-locked province, not a likely place to see a seagull. Given that, I asked her to remain open to the avenue through which the seagull sign would arrive.

Before her daughter stepped back, she brought me the lyrics and the melody to a familiar song. I passed this last message along and let her Mom know that I would find a link to the music and send it to her so that she could listen.

This unexpected back and forth occurred before I had my mandatory cup of morning coffee. I put off finding the song and I headed to the the kitchen. It did not take me long to realize that the spirit had not disconnected from my energy. The daughter's spirit stayed with me while I scooped the coffee grounds into the pot. She seemed to be underfoot; so close that I felt I might trip over her. I abandoned my plans for coffee and surrendered to what she wanted.

I fired up the laptop. When I keyed in the title of the song, many links for the song were listed. Without planning to, I clicked on the first link. What came up, took my breath away – there, on the screen in front of me, was the exact image I had visualized earlier! A young woman on the beach, arms outstretched with many seagulls circling the air above her.

With so many links to choose from, why was that one at the top? Why had I chosen it? Surely this was her mom's sign and it explained why she was so insistent that I send the song right away. The song and the accompanying video brought much comfort to this mother who felt she had lost everything.

Later, as I reflected on this experience, it made me consider how the mental health crisis was compounded during the COVID pandemic. The uncertainty and loss of routine that came with the COVID-19 crisis would only make burdens of depression and anxiety even heavier. The isolation rules prevented parents from travelling to their children; made it even more difficult for concerned family members, like Andrea, to keep watch on their loved ones battling mental illness and addictions.

I find it is often in the darkest shadows that we find our greatest chance for light. And soon, that light began seeping through the cracks that were left behind from this story.... The first tendril of light showed me that my own teenage daughter was struggling under a blanket of depression. With my full permission, she began painting a COVID mural on her bedroom wall, which allowed what was ugly to become beautiful.

The light continued to spread and illuminated my personal past struggles with depression and addictions. My mother never gave up on me during that dark time but recently, when she exited my life briefly, I felt she had. I soon learned that she battled her own mental health issues. Being so moved by this client experience, I began to communicate with my mom again.

There are always going to be sections along the road of life that are full of bumps or broken pieces. But it is at these sacred spots that we are taught to slow down and look for the blessings that are there, too.

A Reading of Clouds*
Chad Norman

Someone says something about a storm.

So I say what better time
to head out for a walk...
my favourite walk.

Each step allows me to see the stones again,
allows me to feel a change
one I only know as a new season.

Each look up at a vocal sky
brings what I hear,
what I question to know a sound
I dare believe is a reading of clouds...
those ones I can't name.

Those ones I see and have seen
many times when my neck needs a workout.

A reading of clouds,
each gust like a language meant for me,
why I've spent a lifetime

seeking what the sky is about
and what I will never be a part of...
left to stare and talk out loud to the wind
about whatever those clouds are named.

Each one, all of them way above
anything I might've been myself,
or the other curious men
I can say are also locked to
and led by unforgettable stories
often written about the land.

* Written between March 12–18 at the Old Road BBQ, Truro, NS during the worldwide outbreak of the Coronavirus.

A Study in Isolation....
Alnoor Rajan Talwar

This poem was inspired by the senseless violence...the shootings in Nova Scotia as well as the racial violence in the USA and in other parts of the world....
We are already suffering the consequences of COVID-19. Violence only makes the present situation even worse.
I wrote this on behalf of the people who have lost someone to the senseless acts of violence.

    Rain tapping
    on my window,
        skies blanketed
        by heavy clouds,
fierce winds of growing concern
bellowing down on my spirit
eroding my sensibilities
                My face,
        kissed by the rosy flush
          of maddening aggravating thoughts...
  ...as we stand proud...
          oblivious to our brutality,
      our ignorance
and our insensitivity...

...conquering, decimating, annihilating
whomever, however, whenever,
in whichever
way we are able to…

Through this,
    I miss you
  every second
      of every minute
          of every hour
              of every day…
And, if I could
miss you more,
I most certainly would

Despite It All
Catherine A. MacKenzie

Amid the darkness
And despair and doom,
View the blazing sun
And azure sky…
Or the silvery moon
And nightly black
When the living rest
After a day of light.

Grasp your hands
And flex your fingers,
Be grateful for
Limbs that move:
Legs to carry
You through the day
And arms to fold
On your chest at night.

Feel blessed for breath
That wakes you
Every morning,
For the power to yawn
And stretch,

To frown
Or smile,
To greet a new day.

In this new normal
Of a not-so-gentle world
Of confusion and chaos
Be kind,
For we share one life.

Be thankful for tears,
For to love is to cry and
To die is to have lived.

Despite doom
And despair
Be grateful
To be alive,
To see the sun
And the moon,
For what is the
Alternative?

Coping With COVID-19

Sylvia Lucas

This isolation is a pain in the butt.

Greg wasn't able to get out to see Sherry, and she had become petulant, as if it were his fault that it had been nearly a week since they'd gotten together. Five days! That's all it had been. Five days of social distancing, or whatever they were calling it now. He hoped his confinement to the house and working from home was not going to last long and that it all lined up as planned. Perhaps this bloody virus would go away, die off, or be dealt with fairly soon....

This life wouldn't be too bad really: no need to get up so early; leisurely breakfasts; working at the computer in the sitting room, quiet and comfortable.... Beats the open-plan madhouse I'm used to.

Sherry was the problem. She took every opportunity to ask when he was coming to see her, and Melanie, well, Melanie was just Melanie. With that stoic acceptance of her lot. Oh! How that drove him mad! It used to seem like an uncomplaining cheerfulness before they were married. Soon he saw it for what it was: a delight in playing the martyr.

Melanie dropped the last tea towel into the washing machine, measured the detergent and poured it slowly over the items in the drum. She thought about the past few days. Not bad for some: all meals and snacks served on time, television and music in the evening, feet up on the recliner and a bowl of popcorn in their lap or a can of lager in hand? Whereas she, Melanie, to achieve that, had twice the work and no time alone for herself.

Did Greg seriously believe she was unaware of his affairs? Three in the three years they'd been married. Of course, there could also have been the odd one night stand here and there, of which she was ignorant, but she had certainly known about Nichola, Sophie and now Sherry. Oh yes! It was easy to spot the symptoms of his infidelity and surprisingly easy to learn more when she assumed a look of gormless innocence. The phone calls. The incessant texting and the mysterious errands. No doubt he would soon offer to get the groceries. That's just how he was. Did he even realize that for him, the grass would always be greener on the other side of the fence? At least until he was old and grey, if he lived that long. Melanie closed the machine, adjusted the settings and pressed the START button.

How Sherry hated this isolation. She'd never liked being alone, and being shut up in a second-floor flat the size of a large shoebox was no fun at all. Not to mention that she missed Greg and worried about him during the COVID-19 pandemic.

She knew he was careful and didn't really worry he would catch the virus – and if he did, he wasn't in a susceptible category for any serious consequences. No, the worry was that, unable to visit her and shut up with his wife, he might be tempted to have sex with Melanie again after all these months. He had assured her that the marriage was over, except for the domestic civilities, but one could never trust men to be celibate for long.

She opened the bathroom cabinet and reached for a box of hair dye. She'd colour her hair and cheer herself up, and if Greg managed to get over to see her she'd be looking her best.

Ten days! Stupid as it was, he'd actually checked the calendar and counted the days one by one! Ten days, and he hadn't set foot out of the house except to put out the rubbish or pick up a parcel from the step. Each time he opened the front door, Melanie called out, "Be sure to wash your hands after you touch the parcel. Online shopping is all very well but things are still packed by people and handled by postal staff," she'd remind him.

That made him feel like a three-year-old being lectured about playing with mud pies! His offers to shop for supplies were met with assurances that their fridge was already well-stocked, as was their freezer and pantry. Melanie gloated over her competency. Damned woman thinks of everything.

No chance of her getting infected….

Or was there?

The thought had come into Greg's head unbidden; at least he was not conscious of any thought process searching for it, or any secret wish leading up to it. The thought simply occurred to him that if Melanie became infected, with her asthma, there was a serious chance that.... What was he thinking? Why even acknowledge the thought?

She did not go out at all. The daycare facility where she normally worked a 24-hour week was closed, as were all schools. Melanie knew she was vulnerable and did not venture out – and risk infection. If she were ever to catch COVID-19, the infection would have to come to her.

This thought led to others, spreading like a virus through Greg's brain. If Melanie fell victim to COVID-19, it would be fate in a way if she passed, and then he would be a free man, able to spend as much time as he liked with Sherry, who never seemed to get enough of him.

Maybe if he'd let the idea simmer away in his mind for a day or two, he would have dismissed it as immoral, illegal or impractical. But, Greg acted on impulse and told Melanie he intended to go to the supermarket for some coffee ice cream.

"I have a sudden mad desire," he told his wife, prompting Melanie to ask if he were pregnant.

Not waiting to give her time to argue, he quickly set off. He wore gloves, the grey woollen ones his Aunt Claire had given him for Christmas. They would give him some protection, but he also rubbed them along trolley handles, and any other surface he thought would have been handled by many people.

Carefully afterwards, Greg dropped the gloves into a plastic bag where they remained until he arrived back home. Then he set about contaminating various items Melanie was likely to touch: her hairbrush, her jewellery box, her makeup case.

Once started, his actions gained a momentum of their own, and Greg repeated the process on several occasions. Weeks passed. Melanie remained well, however Sherry was not quite so fortunate. Am I responsible? He questioned himself when Sherry texted him the bad news. His frequent forays out into the world at large, and his snatched hours now and then with Sherry, might have backfired. Still, Greg wasn't worried about her. Sherry was young and healthy, he thought; it was just a nuisance for her.

Greg was wrong. Sherry had an undiagnosed heart condition and became gravely ill. The doctors believed it might never have been a problem, but under the circumstances, it was fatal.

Melanie read the news of Sherry's death in the local paper.

She did her best to console Greg, although the matter was never actually spoken of.

Greg realized Melanie was always there for him and would be; she was kind, efficient and an all-around good wife. He should settle down and appreciate her more. How could he have harboured such evil thoughts?

Still, there was no harm done.

Melanie carefully sanitized all her things regularly, particularly when Greg had been out. He was given to rash actions but Greg wasn't really a bad man. Things would settle down; they would be okay.

He was subdued now, and feeling contrite. But, of course, Melanie knew he'd continue to have affairs, even if he didn't think he would at this moment. And she would cope, as she'd always done. Melanie knew what she wanted: a quiet ordered life, but she also wanted Greg, which tended to complicate matters somewhat. Things usually worked out, though sometimes they needed a bit of a nudge.

Had Sherry seriously believed Greg had been thoughtful enough to leave a parcel containing that lovely Easter egg outside her door? The card addressed to "My Easter Bunny" was not only romantic, Melanie had decided, it also allowed for no signature, or any possible pet name used between them.

Aunt Claire's grey wool gloves, secretly appropriated when Greg's attention was elsewhere, had done their work.

Fate had just needed a nudge, after all.

Breathe

Bonnie L. Baird

it takes the breath away....

desks gathering dust in cubed-off spaces
the air above conference tables stilled
no phones ringing

you can hear yourself breathe

we left so fast, some of us
when will we be back?

will we be back?

indeterminate days and nights for some
hours and skills shift with need

when will the need be met?

the washer spins while we shower before we greet our kids:
are they safe?
Breathe

it's still coming, not yet upon us
fully

tracking world stats: the latest addiction
Breathe

the guard outside the store
posted limits

no swings move except in the wind

the lack of touch

the one who still doesn't get it stands
not a hockey stick away
but right next
and how did that come to feel so odd so fast?

taillights that flashed unbroken down the road you overlook
from your apartment
occasional
now
and where are they going?
Breathe

birds are singing
we can hear them
people too across empty courtyards
fish swim in undisturbed waters
the muck is settling

candles lit in windows
laments and thanks rise
for so much
not noticed before
Breathe

through the mask that keeps others safe
upon the screen that shows
a parent or child we cannot hold
Breathe

in this isolated space
separate, yet together

breathe out, breathe in
Breathe

LOVE CONQUERS ALL
Mary Anne White

"She's just getting out of the shower. Here she is," my husband said as he handed me the phone. I wondered what could possibly be so important.

"Hi, Auntie Mary Anne." My nephew in San Francisco was calling me for the first time in his 28 years. My heart flipped, as I imagined trouble. "I called to say we're getting married next weekend. I didn't want to send you an email invitation without giving you some context."

My nephew and his fiancée met working in San Francisco, although they were both from Canada and graduates from the same Canadian university. They had been engaged for a year. The last I had heard from my sister, the couple had not settled on wedding plans, a decision complicated by different cultural backgrounds, and a parent who was unable to travel. We had expected to learn details at an engagement party in Canada in April, but that event had been called off due to COVID-19. No update had been mentioned until now. "We are getting married here in San Francisco on Zoom."

When my husband and I married, we followed a traditional route: church wedding with 100 guests. Our biggest departure from custom was brown tuxedos, with orange trim on the men's shirts to match the orange bridesmaids' dresses. What can I say? It was the 1970s.

Weddings of an even earlier era commonly took place without many family members or friends, due to circumstances of war or difficulties in travel, or family conflict, at least according to the Jimmy Stewart movies we have been watching while physically distancing. We now realize that big blowout weddings are a recent invention. And these pandemic times lead to fresh ways to do things, even if they really are old ways repackaged.

Our nephew's was not the first wedding we had attended with an email invitation, but, as a marker of our times, it is worth capturing:

> **Subject: We are Getting Married!**
>
> Hey! You may have noticed the world's been going through a weird phase lately. We hope you are able to take a break from all of that to celebrate something exciting with us.
>
> "We're getting married this Saturday! We hope you can find time between baking sourdough and watching Tiger King to join us online.
>
> We'll be bringing a few friends and family members to the park with us to share some vows, sign some paperwork, all hosted on a Zoom call with you lovely people!
>
> Sign in, put yourselves on mute, and celebrate with us.
>
> Attire: Tuxedo, PJs, or whatever you want

And they did get married, on a sunny afternoon in a verdant garden. Yes, the park was officially closed, and the attendance exceeded the allowed gathering size by one person. And just as the ceremony began, another aunt accidentally shared her computer screen on Zoom, holding up the proceedings. Not many newlyweds can claim that kind of wedding interruption!

All around the world, from North America to Israel to China, nearly 300 people watched on Zoom or WeChat. We all had front row seats. A cousin from New Orleans played her cello in real time as pre-ceremony music while we flipped through to see many familiar faces. Another cousin, a paramedic, was in his ambulance in full gear, ready in case of a call. The groom's parents and sister were at home on their couch, champagne in hand. Our own children and their families were there in their homes, four time zones from us. The remote guests had taken the attire request to heart, literally from tuxedo to PJs. My husband and I were dressed up too, at least from the waist up. At the last minute, I blew the dust off my Chanel No. 5 and gave myself a spritz: This was the first event that I had attended in a decade that was not scent-free. We sat at our dining table in Halifax with hors d'oeuvres and wine, ready to celebrate.

It was a beautiful wedding. The ceremony was short and to the point, emphasizing how much the bride and groom both value their families. Their vows were especially touching, highlighting how each was completed by their life partner. My glasses fogged up.

After the ceremony was over, we had a chance to chat and catch up on pandemic life in each of the participant's locations. In typical Canadian fashion, many of us complained of the fickle spring weather. We saw children in far-flung places who we had not yet met in person. We really felt connected. And an hour after it started, it was over and, given our Atlantic time zone, we went off to bed.

The next day I had a follow-up chat with several family members and the post-wedding excitement was in the air, as if we had been there in person. We all commented that we were neither hungover nor worn out from dancing. It was a given that we missed more personal interactions and our traditional family group photos; we were attempting to look on the sunny side.

In our family, we like to analyse impacts. My sister, with a mind for business, had estimated the economic effect of the Zoom wedding. With no one flying, no hotel stays, no new clothes, no wedding reception, no rehearsal dinner, no showers, and no stag parties, her guess was that half a million dollars stayed in our collective pockets. Thinking of the loss to businesses, the newlyweds asked for donations to charity instead of gifts. It took us no time at all to decide to send their traditional gift money to Feed Nova Scotia.

As a scientist, my thoughts turned to the environmental impact. I estimated the greenhouse gases not emitted on account of 300 guests staying home: about 500 metric tonnes of CO_2 equivalent. To put it in context, the absence of flown-in guests for the wedding was like taking about 100 cars off the road for a year. Of course, the price we are all paying for the pandemic is high in many other ways.

Why did they not wait to marry later?

The bride expressed the reasons for the Zoom wedding in her vows: "I honestly can't think of a worse time to get married, all things considered, but somehow we've managed to make these COVID times a sort of adventure in its own way. I have learned that if we can make an adventure out of these times then I really can't wait to see what our life will look like." And the no-fuss Zoom wedding allowed the young couple to focus on their main goal – being married.

This is a new world now, with new ways of doing things as we go forward. We will all remember 2020 as a pivot point, a time Joan Baez predicted as The Great Correction. But people will still fall in love and want to commit themselves to each other, witnessed by family and friends, COVID-19 be damned.

First appeared in The Globe and Mail.

Now Easter Comes
Bonnie L Baird

now Easter comes
not by calendar but in essence

doors flung open
each of us out of our private spaces
restricted, monitored no more

first light and first touch of a friend's hand

face to face, unmasked

coffee poured in cafes
the hum of conversations all around
leaning in to hear what's being said

sitting side by side on a bench
in a park
or alone on a bench while others walk by
unmeasured

weight of a dying beloved's hand in yours
while you whisper close

"It's okay to go home. We'll be okay."
honouring that life with others

dust accumulated in libraries, shops
swept away

a drive along the shore with a son who lives away

checking on patients without being afraid
washrooms and showers and restaurants open
for the long haul

a grandchild's bear hug

potlucks
big-screen movies and live concerts
packed in together

hard pews and music that speaks to the soul
light filtered through stained glass, old scriptures
prayers rising together

now Easter comes
in the minutia of everyday living
seen for what it really is:
gift
pure gift

A Long, Long-Term Lockdown

Louise Piper

"To live is the rarest thing. Most people exist, that is all."
– Oscar Wilde

In March, my daughter and her boyfriend were celebrating her birthday in New York. I was at work with too much time on my hands since the lady I am a companion to, whom I shall name Marion, was playing bridge with some of her friends in the retirement facility where they all live.

Around the card table, the ladies were lamenting that their sons and daughters were rethinking plans to visit, concerned that the airport and flights from another province might be too risky. My mind wandered to my daughter – she was due to fly to her home in Ireland the following day. Would the flight still run? Would the borders still be open to allow her flight to land?

That evening, Prime Minister Justin Trudeau announced that he was closing the Canadian borders. It had started with some of the smaller provinces declaring a state of emergency in the previous days and weeks. But now our worst fears had been confirmed – COVID-19 had reached our shores.

During those early days, Marion and I would watch the daily television briefings. COVID was certainly west of us. And north of us. Those provinces had already declared a state of emergency. More worrisome, south of the border, cases were rising at an alarming rate. What would this mean for us all?

Marion has mobility issues and relies on a series of carers to help her through the day. She needs help getting up in the morning, getting dressed and going to the washroom. Bright and mentally agile, she also needs intellectual stimulus. What would this pandemic mean for Marion?

As COVID-19 spread with alacrity, our worlds shrank overnight. I had said goodbye to Marion and told her I would see her the following day. By the time I reached home, a state of emergency had been declared in our province, Nova Scotia. Seniors' homes were in lockdown. It would be eight weeks before I would be able to see Marion again.

In that time, I would send her photos and emails and leave her sweet treats at a drop-off point in the facility. These were tenuous attempts to sustain our connection, but I knew this was not nearly enough to meet Marion's needs.

To keep their residents safe, the retirement facility suspended visits from family, friends, external carers and companions. More than this, the large communal dining space the residents enjoyed was closed. Dressing for formal dinner had been one of the highlights of each day for Marion. Now residents were required to take their meals on their own floors. This was a significant disappointment to Marion since her close friends resided on other floors.

The residents' bridge meetings, group exercise classes and film screenings stopped. All Marion could do was sit in her room.

Alone. In this regard, her experience of lockdown was similar to many people's outside of the facility. Except that most of us were able to explore new ways to occupy ourselves, even within our homes.

I would exercise in my lounge in front of YouTube. I continued my writing workshops via Zoom which also facilitated sharing cooking and baking experiences with members of my family locked-down in their own homes. For some of us, the cessation of our former routines allowed us some time for quiet reflection and philosophical musings.

Marion's degenerative disease, however, did not allow her to partake in these kinds of activities, except perhaps for the latter. She had plenty of time to contemplate her own curtailed existence which she has likened to being kept a prisoner. For her, it was a lockdown in the strictest sense of the word.

There seems to be an irony in the fact that while we have been shielding the most vulnerable, aging members of our society, we have diminished their potential for connection to others and shared experience just at that period in their lives when they are wanting to seize as many of these opportunities as they can.

Certainly Marion seemed to resent that such a strict regime was imposed upon her. She felt very isolated and very powerless. Yes, we all did our bit and "stayed the blazes home," and it was this common cause that helped Marion to endure those long, lonely days.

While I was able to walk for fresh air and use my common sense, avoiding any busy areas or crossing the street if I saw someone coming the other way, Marion was denied this choice. Quite honestly, without being able to have those moments to escape the four walls, I'm quite sure I would have slipped into a depressive and anxious state. I worried for Marion's mental well-being.

After a couple of months, I was allowed to resume my visits to her. Strict procedures were in place to ensure the facility remained free of COVID-19. I was asked a series of questions before I began each shift to determine whether I may have potentially been at risk of exposure to the virus. My temperature would be taken and I was required to change into indoor clothes and to wear full PPE.

I would arrive at Marion's room, wearing a long yellow gown that skirted my ankles, large plastic goggles, and a medical mask. Looking like an alien, I would sit with her to play a game of cribbage or Scrabble!

Marion hated that I had to wear the PPE. It was a barrier to protect us both, of course. But it was also a barrier to effective communication. Marion has hearing difficulties and the mask muffled my voice. Furthermore, the mask and goggles concealed my facial expressions and inhibited subtler means of understandings between us.

Gradually, the restrictions began to ease and I was allowed to take Marion out of the facility to get some fresh air. Marion patiently waited while I removed the PPE and changed back into my outdoor clothes. We both wore masks for the duration of our outdoor jaunts which were limited to a walk around the block. It was such a delight for us both to see the cherry blossoms and feel the warmth of the sun on our faces.

Shops began to slowly reopen and the streets became busier. But Marion was not permitted to enter any shops and she found this incredibly frustrating. Once, we were out on a hot, sunny day.

Marion had brought her purse with her. She was clearly on a mission.

It turned out that Marion really fancied having an ice cream. And why not? But we weren't allowed to go into the shops. Marion huffed and waved her hand dismissively as I reminded her of this. I felt caught in a dilemma. I wanted to keep Marion safe, but I also felt guilty denying her such a modest request.

And then we both saw an ice-cream stall. They were serving people on the street so, technically, we wouldn't be entering a shop. Still I wavered, but Marion was resolute. I reasoned that we wouldn't be breaking any provincial guidelines so positioned Marion in an isolated spot while I made the transaction with the ice-cream vendor.

We sat in companionable silence underneath a shady tree and devoured our ice-creams which seemed manna from heaven, a taste of normalcy, a reminder of life's simple pleasures.

When I wheeled Marion back into the facility, the receptionist took our temperature before allowing us in. Fortunately, she didn't comment on the smear of ice-cream on Marion's medical mask!

Marion has explained to me that the worst part of lockdown was being confined to her room day after day. The community aspect of the facility had disappeared overnight. This left Marion feeling incredibly isolated, bored and lonely.

The saddest part of lockdown for me was knowing that Marion, sociable and mischievous, had no way to express that side of her personality. Recently, I asked her to describe her attitude to risk. She told me: "You have to take risks. I suppose I'm a bit of a rebel."

Of course, I had already realized that the day she insisted we buy an ice cream.

Yes, all of our lives have been impacted by this pandemic. For most of us, however, we have been able to gauge the risk of particular situations, and we retain an element of choice in terms of our interpretation of the guidelines. For Marion, she had no choice but to stop living, in a sense. During the COVID lockdown she just existed, like a hibernating animal, long enough for the threat of the virus to diminish so that others could help her to start living her life again.

The Gift of Fear

Bethana Sullivan

When word of COVID-19 began to reach us I found myself anticipating how this virus could affect us and the communities along the eastern shore. What would be needed? Food, gas, physical and emotional support, rides, these were some areas of their lives where people might need help. And who or what agencies would step up, I wondered. But early on there wasn't much coming out on social media and in the paper. Having worked in self-help I set up a Musquodoboit Harbour + Area Community Helpers Facebook page. In no time there were many helpers signed on. This kept me busy for the first month and all of us worked hard to be positive, and supportive. It was a vibrant time and still is.

But one day in late April I woke up lethargic, with a heaviness in my bones. I couldn't shake it no matter what I did – eventually I sat down to write what was in my body and this poem emerged. It is a lament as well as a song of hope. It is a reminder to me that if emotions swing too far one way or another, for any length of time, we need to pay attention to the unseen and the unspoken.

The Gift of Fear

Bethana Sullivan

Heart full of grief
with feet standing at the edge of the ocean
touching all the world
beyond where the waves
roll out to the horizon.
The heart grieves for long-ago losses
the details no longer rooted to this life.
The body remembers time gone by
and so cradles itself in sunlight sparkling over the trees.
We, too, face being cut down
without warning, like the forests around us.
We, too, might join the litany of losses
of life from this world.

Our hearts grieve and we are laid low.
Our bodies laboriously lumber through the day.
All around us fear overwhelms
while we reach out to help
to shore up the walls that hold the darkness out.
What lurks there to frighten us so?
Is it fear of death, of loss so overwhelming

that the heart will collapse in on herself?
Of being alone?
That no one will love us...?
That we are vulnerable to the unexpected?

This time is a great reminder
of what lies beneath our fear.
The stuff we do not want to look at or feel
rises up like a tsunami, flooding the plains of everyday life.
The desire is to protect and shelter
from what we cannot control.
And the earth is denied the tears
that moisten the soil of our body.
Today's grief washes over us, through us
and we feel the tears wet the dry places,
run into the cracks of our bodies
where grit has collected
washing out, and cleansing the wounds of what is....

I stand, my flat feet gripping the floor
and I go to the place where fear lurks,
into the always wild unknown
one slow footstep at a time.

Step, stop, breathe.
Step, stop, breathe.

And I sense the footsteps of my ancestors
tilling the fields in their hunger
seeding them with their hope.
And I hear stomping footsteps
coming to push them out.

And I see ships sailing
away from the known shore.

Step, stop, breathe.
Step, stop, breathe.

And I hear the sound of singing
all 'round the dinner table.
And I see the bright-faced children
running freely everywhere.
And I feel the welcome of strangers
on this new, unknown shore.

Step, stop, breathe.
Step, stop, breathe.

And I see the darkness coming
and I know that it will pass.
For we are more than our minds remember
as our ancestors' resilience carries on.

OLYGYOLOGY
Alnoor Rajan Talwar

this daily deluge
       of bad news
              is the reason for
                     my vocabularical inventoluge…
…wimpology, groanology, angerology, disgustology,
          anxietology, hopeology and of course, faithology

as i go through this isological evolution
       of catastrophical proportion,
             crazology is aplenty
                    and my inventology,
                     the only feasible solution

i do not speak…(there is nobody to speak to)
              …i squeak and shriek with delightology
              oh my!
            i am the squeakological inventologist!
(…and they said i'd never amount to anything!)

This was an attempt and an experiment in using "creative license" and bring some humour to my fears and reactions to all the negativity around us.

SURVIVAL: HERE I AM!
Chad Norman – for Nicoleta

My foot in a favourite slipper
taps just above the carpet
installed years ago,
across the room filled
with the songs of Bad Co.
making me cry,
feel for the days I was 15.

Here I am back with Mystery
or am I moving ahead
holding its hand not knowing
a thing about the future,
standing nonetheless on "Only,"
a place I was afraid of,
standing though, only, only, only...?

Steps continue to be effective
one, still after, one, how to
be about survival, how
I will survive again, moving
still, an older man I want,
an older thought of who he is,

or, perhaps, an older me now ready
for the newness I know nothing about.

I see the bird feeder is being soiled.
I revere the birds unafraid of the storm.

Here I am,
asking for nothing,
with no hands brought to a prayer.
Here I am
setting out to help the crows
who always have an answer first.

100 Days
Brent Sedo

We were three weeks from the end of our annual four-month winter on the South Pacific shores of Mexico when things took a turn. To an extent isolated from the real world, this COVID-19 problem was something that was happening far away in other places to other people, not effecting our little village at all.

Then one day in mid-March we hear the prime minister of Canada is making an important announcement, and we bring up the CBC on the computer. In a somber tone he's speaking to Canadians like us, scattered around the globe, telling us that borders are closing, airlines are shutting down, and "it's time to come home."

Okay, we're coming, in three weeks. We take stock of the situation, weigh the pros and cons. We're fortunate that we own our house there, no worries about paying additional rent or being evicted from a hotel. We have good neighbours who have become good friends and we all look out for each other. Our tourist visas are valid until June. And perhaps most significant of all, there is no word from the airline that our flight is going to be cancelled. To the contrary, checking the website indicates they are still selling tickets for it.

We decide to sit tight, stick to the plan, assume we'll be leaving as scheduled. Besides, the president of Mexico has also been on TV, and in a decidedly not-somber tone he's told the Mexican people not to be afraid, to live life as normal, go out, eat, drink, hug and kiss your compadres. Keep the economy going. For his part, he's counting on religious amulets to keep him safe. To prove the point, he pulls them out of his pocket and shows them to the cameras.

So really, how bad can it be?

We start a daily check of the airline, the flight remains available, tickets are still being sold. One day we get notification there has been a slight alteration to the flight schedule, but the e-mail assures us there have been no other changes. Two weeks to go and we remain confident, start to take our usual steps to close up the house, arrange for it to be cleaned and the garden looked after when we leave.

And then one morning I come down to the kitchen, pour myself a cup of coffee, and my wife informs me she received another e-mail from the airline in the middle of the night. Our flight, the one they were selling tickets for the day before, has been cancelled.

I take my coffee outside, take a sip and then look up just in time to see a gray whale a couple hundred metres offshore, completely out of the water and horizontal. A huge splash and it's gone. I watch for a few minutes but it doesn't resurface.

The immediate concern is that we are just a few days from the start of Semana Santa, Easter week, one of the biggest holiday times in

Mexico when all the small towns along our stretch of the coast are overrun with tourists, mostly from Mexico City. If they bring the virus here it will be a big problem. The local public hospital, serving a region of more than 50,000 people, doesn't even have an ICU, let alone ventilators. There's one doctor in the next village over who spends most of his time treating sunstroke and Montezuma's revenge. He's completely unequipped to handle what might come. But thankfully, the local government springs into action (not a common occurrence in Mexico) and decisions start to be handed down. Restaurants and hotels will close. Construction sites will be shut down. The road into and out of our neighbouring villages will be barricaded to allow access to residents only, and we'll need a pass to get in and out. Only vendors providing essential services – drinking water, gas for cooking, fruits and vegetables – will be allowed in. For now, at least, we are saved. The barbarians will be kept beyond the gates.

The second concern is for the hundreds of local people who are suddenly out of work. The contrast is glaring. In the news from Canada, it seems almost daily the government announces another multi-billion-dollar financial aid package for another group of people. People suddenly unemployed because of the virus will get money. People whose businesses have been closed because of the virus will get money. Students will get money. Seniors will get money. No one is left out.

For the people of rural Mexico who survive day to day as construction labourers or restaurant staff or selling boat tours on the beach, there is nothing like that. They will simply have to tough it out for however long it takes.

We assure Francesca, our cleaning lady who comes once-a-week for a half day and earns the equivalent of $15 Canadian, we will continue to pay her even though she lives some distance away on the other side of the barricade and can't actually come to clean. The problem is getting her the money. She doesn't have a bank account to e-mail it to, she wouldn't know what PayPal even is. One day on the phone she tells my wife she's making and selling tortillas to try and make ends meet.

In the final days before the blockades go up we decide to make the 45-minute run to the one large grocery store in the area to stock up on supplies. It turns out to be a good decision as we don't get back there for almost three months.

With a long list in hand we grab a cart and navigate the store, concentrating on fancy non-staples we know we won't be able to find in the small, family-run shops in our village.

With the future uncertain, we take two of almost everything. Nearly an hour later we join the checkout line, and slowly it dawns on us – none of the Mexicans in line with us are buying more than a few items each. A young mother with a loaf of bread, a bag of tomatoes and some dish-washing soap. An older gentleman has instant coffee, corn flour and vegetable oil. We, on the other hand, have smoked sausage and imported cheese and bottles of red wine, and our cart is so full it threatens to spill over onto the floor. No one in front of us spends more than a couple hundred pesos. When it's all added up, we spend more than 3000. We head for the door, feeling embarrassed by our riches.

And then we settle in to wait. My wife teaches both her university classes and her yoga classes online and finds that she enjoys it. I do some writing assignments and tackle fix-it-up jobs around the house. We play lots of cribbage and Yahtzee and watch dark European crime dramas on Netflix. Except for the lack of people – and one scary week when the local shops completely run out of beer and wine – life in the village continues pretty much as normal. Time passes rather quickly. We measure it out Saturday to

Saturday, because that's when Francesca would normally come, and now we're doing the cleaning ourselves. More than once we look at each other and say, "Doesn't it seem like we just did this a couple days ago?"

We follow the news from Canada, and find we're relieved we are missing out on what appears to be a lot of stress and anxiety. Friends and family keep us informed about the ongoing debates over mask-wearing, the constant vigilance with social distancing (and the social shaming that goes along with it), the strict adherence to staying home and in your small bubble of immediate family.

Our bubble is the entire village. Social distancing isn't really a thing; the only people who wear masks are the vendors who are allowed to travel in and out, and we continue to get together with small groups of friends, just like the president of Mexico said we should (although we do avoid hugging and kissing). Visa status notwithstanding, we could stay here for the whole summer, and even float the idea of staying on right through to the next winter season.

But the one nagging thought is that our extended health insurance coverage for any COVID-19-related illness has been cancelled and if the virus does come for us, we could be in trouble. And we wouldn't want to take scant health care resources from the Mexican people who might need it. Eventually we have to go and in late May we start looking for flights.

It's not easy. One airline informs us on their website that due to a high volume of calls, wait times on the phone could be up to 500 minutes. Apparently that sounds better than eight hours. We find one airline that over and over issues us tickets for flights they cancel one week later. We end up with future travel credit at three different airlines. For a while it looks like we'll be leaving on July 1, which my wife thinks would be appropriate, but then that flight is cancelled as well.

Finally, we get a date that sticks. July 12, exactly 100 days after our original departure date. We start to slowly pack up a couple days before, both thinking the same thing. Despite everything, we don't really want to leave.

Through the initial flight to Mexico City, the overnight in a hotel, the second flight to Toronto, the third flight to Halifax, we're plunged into all the stress and anxiety we had missed out on: the constant reminders to wear a mask; the continuous announcements to maintain distance (impossible on an airplane); the signage everywhere warning of the ever-present threat that the virus is hanging around.

Now in our Nova Scotia house on the lake, we think of what the prime minister said on that day in mid-March, and it occurs to us that maybe our home, our real world, is what we left down there in Mexico.

And we wonder when we'll be able to get back to it.

Contributor Bios

Ruth Ann Adams

Ruth Ann Adams is a high school English teacher, pastor's wife, mother of five and grandma of one. She has been published in magazines and anthologies, including *Hot Apple Cider with Cinnamon: Stories of Finding Love in Unexpected Places*, edited by N.J. Lindquist. Ruth Ann has a blog named "5 X Mama" at ruthannadams.com. She belongs to both local and national writers' groups.

Ruth Ann is addicted to cats and British history. She is passionate about sharing encouragement and hope with others. Ruth Ann is from Owen Sound, Ontario, on Georgian Bay, and has lived in the beautiful province of Nova Scotia for 20 years.

Bonnie L. Baird

Bonnie Baird is a poet and writer of postcard stories. She has published five books of poetry and one book of short stories, and is currently working on a fictional memoir. Other passions include walking, spending time with her grandchildren and friends and cat, and pastoral ministry. Though her home now is in Bedford, her heart will always belong to Nova Scotia's South Shore, ancestral home and place where she has lived and worked.

Bonnie's published works include these: *Walk Me to the Door, Love* (notes written to the Beloved in the first two years of grief) – also available as CD; *I Smell Stars* (final twelve years of a marriage) – also available as CD; *Lightning Strikes* (reflections on complicated family relationships); *Close to the Undertow* (poems on the experience of ministry); *Songs in the Night* (poems for use in the church and of lamentation); *Survival of the Dangly Green Parrot Earrings* (short stories on ministry).

JANET BARKHOUSE

Janet Barkhouse's poems and stories have been published across Canada in such journals as *CV2*, *Literary Review of Canada*, *Riddle Fence*, *Room*, *TNQ*, and in anthologies, including *My Nova Scotia Home* (MacIntyre Purcell 2019), *Aubade* (Boularderie 2018), *Whispers of Mermaids and Wonderful Things* (Nimbus 2017). Her debut collection of poems, *Salt Fires*, published by Pottersfield Press in the fall of 2018, follows on two chapbooks, *Silence* and *Sable Island Fieldnotes* (with photographs by Zoe Lucas); a "docupoem" short film screened at Lunenburg Doc Fest 2017; and three children's books. She lives in Mi'kma'ki, near Mahone Bay on Nova Scotia's South Shore.

MELANIE DONNELLY

Melanie Donnelly, a singer/songwriter from N.B., has travelled and performed across Canada, Australia and Scotland, finally settling in Nova Scotia. She co-wrote a number of songs including "Stand Together" which received an honorable mention in the American Songwriter Contest and "We'll Find A Way," a musical green initiative in which all proceeds went to environmental organizations. Melanie also performed back-up vocals for several local artists such as Hal Bruce, John Morgan, Eileen Joyce and Frank MacKay. She wrote and recorded her own songs with producer/engineer Ross Billard and several others with Scott Ferguson and Hal Bruce, which were put together on a CD entitled Multiplicity. Several years later, working with songwriter and producer, William Crowdis and producer, Donnie Chapman, Melanie compiled another collection of works and recorded the CD Wherever Goes which included songs like "Wherever Goes" and "Light the Lantern," revealing the influence of living life on the East Coast.

DYLAN B. FASSBENDER

A pseudonym used to protect Dylan's identity.

Dylan is well-educated and used to live life in the fast lane. He has retired from that life in favour of pursuing a life-long passion for storytelling and writing.

At one time Dylan had intense exposure to music, media, art, and technology and completed his Fine Arts Degree at a prestigious school in his home city of Halifax. He also studied screen writing, film production and media arts. Now, as a writer, Dylan takes a sharp, honest, and painful look deep into the shallow worlds that few people experience.

KATHY FRANCE

Kathy France is a theatre artist and writer living in Wolfville, Nova Scotia. Originally from Winnipeg, Ms. France spent 17 years living as an expat in exotic locales, including Syria, Yugoslavia, Trinidad, Thailand and Nepal.

While overseas, she worked as a playwright, director, actress and theatre educator and founded her theatre company, Caravan Theatre, which she figured was an apropos name for a company that kept moving from country to country. Her plays have been produced and performed in numerous countries. Ms. France seeks to engage audiences' minds and sprits in theatre that is innovative and inspirational. She works with emerging and established theatre, dance and music artists to explore disparate ideas, forms and styles in found and original material.

With her return to Canada, Ms. France continues to explore her passion for writing. She enjoys writing spoken-word performance pieces, and is currently working on a travel memoir.

CYNTHIA FRENCH

Cynthia French lives in Newburne, Nova Scotia with her husband, Les and dog, Laddie. She has published in *CV2, Riddle Fence, The New Quarterly*, and *Literary Review of Canada*; the anthologies *The Wild Weathers, Untying the Apron: Daughters Remember Mothers of the 1950s* and *Aubade*; and online sites such as *The League of Canadian Poets*. She is an associate editor for *ARC Poetry Magazine*. Cynthia has attended writing workshops from places as diverse as Tatamagouche, Fredericton, Sable River, Lockport, Banff, Sage Hill, Halifax, Mahone Bay, Chile and Greece but still has a lot to learn.

She has come to love Nova Scotia as fiercely as she does her home province of Newfoundland and extends her sympathy to all those affected by COVID-19 and the horrendous massacre which led to this poem. Also condolences to all of us who now believe we should lock our doors.

DOROTHY GRANT

Dorothy Grant enjoyed several careers during her "working years" – each of them truly fulfilling. First, she graduated from the Halifax Infirmary nursing school, and once worked at the famous Roosevelt Hospital in New York, then she was a consumer reporter with both CBC radio and television in Halifax and in her final role, was Director of

Communications with what was then, The Medical Society of Nova Scotia.

All the while, she nurtured an irrepressible passion for writing and has written and published two books and literally hundreds of articles, reports etc. in countless publications. Now semi-retired, she continues to "exploit" her Apple computer in order to, hopefully produce some fascinating material/articles etc. people will want to read!

CHAYA GRATTO

Chaya Gratto is a shamanic reiki practitioner and medium for spirit. She is passionate about guiding others through profound inner growth and personal healing. Her own grief recovery inspired her to leave her career as a corporate trainer and return to her true path: healing work. She has certifications in Adler Coaching, Jikiden Reiki, Aromatouch therapy and completed a year of "Spirit Talker" training under renowned Mi'kmaq medium, Shawn Leonard. She has a diploma in Shamanic Energy Healing and is currently enrolled in a one-year Medicine Woman apprenticeship. Her desire to lead with purpose has extended to facilitating women's circles and being guest speaker at a Wine, Women & Well-Being event. Chaya finds joy in singing, writing and walking barefoot through the forest. She lives in beautiful St. Margaret's Bay with her four children – her greatest teachers. Learn more at www.chayagratto.com or follow her on Facebook at facebook.com/chayagratto/

DAVID HUEBERT

David Huebert is a writer of fiction, poetry and essays from Halifax, Mi'kma'ki. David's work has won the CBC Short Story Prize, *The Walrus* Poetry Prize, and was a National Magazine Award nominee (fiction) in 2018 and 2019. David's fiction debut, *Peninsula Sinking*, won a Dartmouth Book Award, was shortlisted for the Alistair MacLeod Short Fiction Prize, and was runner-up for the Danuta Gleed Literary Award.

David's poems, stories and essays have been published in magazines such as *The Walrus*, *enRoute*, and *Canadian Notes & Queries*, and anthologized in *Best Canadian Stories*. His second collection of poems, *Humanimus*, will be published in the fall of 2020. David is currently working on a new collection of short stories and a YA novel, *Sick Harbour*, co-written with Sarah Sawler.

JAN FANCY HULL

Jan Fancy Hull lives beside a quiet lake in Lunenburg County, where she has written her debut non-fiction book *Where's Home?* as well as poetry and fiction.

Published by Moose House Publications in the summer of 2020, *Where's Home?* explores the many ways Nova Scotians experience home, or wish they did. Home is not always as it seems. Or as expected. Or attainable.

Jan Fancy Hull has previously published an essay in *The Chronicle Herald*, a short story in *The Antigonish Review*, and a poem to accompany the cover photo of her group of sculptures, "The Sentinels," also in *The Antigonish Review*. A collection of her works of short fiction is currently under review for publication.

When not writing, Jan served in various careers, enterprises, pursuits, and avocations, including arts administrator, sailing tours skipper, and employee-benefits broker. Now retired – from earning a living – she carves sculptures from Nova Scotia sandstone, is involved in the Lunenburg Art Society, and writes.

She is on Facebook as Jan Fancy Hull and Jan Hull Stoneist. Websites: janfancyhull.ca / thestoneist.com

Dr. Gregory V. Loewen

One of Canada's leading researchers in ethics, education, aesthetics, health and social theory, G.V. Loewen is the author of forty books and was professor of the interdisciplinary human sciences for two decades in Canada and the USA. He has a quarter century of field research experience including UFO cults, theatrical organizations, artists, health researchers, HR executives and management as well as historical reenactors. His eleven-volume adventure saga, *Kristen-Seraphim*, is the first epic narrative that points beyond the morality and metaphysics of Western consciousness and subverts both the meanings and roles of traditional fantasy elements. He was for eight years in mid-executive management positions in both higher education and corrections. He has consulted for three years in addictions, anxiety and youth and family conflict, practices a version of Daseinanalyse, holds a world top-40 Ph.D. in the human sciences – UBC – and has won over 100K in publication grants and research awards.

Sylvia Lucas

Sylvia Lucas was born in London, England in 1933. She worked in the construction industry in various capacities before moving to Cornwall with her husband and young son. She spent some years renting holiday accommodation before turning a hobby into a business and duplicating audio cassettes and CDs , having a small record label and acting as a booking agent. Retirement, and the move to Nova Scotia followed, and this allowed time for writing short stories. Sylvia says that on the South Shore, she has found her spiritual home.

Catherine A. MacKenzie

Cathy's works appear in print and online, including short story compilations, poetry collections and children's picture books.

She published her first novel, *Wolves Don't Knock*, in 2018. *Mister Wolfe* will be available in 2020, and *My Brother, the Wolf*, the last in the series, in 2021. *Wolves Don't Knock* is available from the author or on

Amazon: https://www.amazon.com/Wolves-Dont-Knock-C-MacKenzie/dp/1927529387

Cathy also edits, formats print and e-books, and publishes other authors under her imprint, MacKenzie Publishing. She lives in West Porters Lake, Nova Scotia, Canada.
Reach out to her at: writingwicket@gmail.com
Check out her website
at: www.writingwicket.wordpress.com

JENNIE MCGUIRE

Jennie McGuire is a multi media artist. She completed Art School and post-grad Art Therapy training in Vancouver (1976).

Jennie likes to push the limits in her exploration of media, colour and abstraction. She sees art as self reflection inspired by the changing vistas of life, nature and travel.

Jennie works out of Tirnanog Studio, Chester, Nova Scotia.

BEVERLEY MCINNES – RUSTWORKS

Beverley was one of 37 Nova Scotia Women Artists to exhibit "Diverse Perspectives" in celebration of the 10th anniversary of the United Nations Decade for Women at Mount St. Vincent University, Nova Scotia.

She organized the stitching of "Kneelers" for All Saints

Cathedral, Halifax and also St. Matthews United Church, Halifax, Tapestry Project depicting its 250-year-old history. She marketed Needlepoint kits for Les Femmes Acadiennes de Clare, NS.

Beverley was the Fort Anne Heritage Tapestry Coordinator for Parks Canada – Fort Anne, Annapolis Royal, NS and supervised the stitching of the tapestry (over 150 square feet) depicting the 400-year history of Fort Anne, Annapolis County and European settlement in Nova Scotia.

Working presently in Rust Assemblages she exhibits both locally and nationally. Her Rustwork installations may be seen presently at White Point Lodge, Whitepoint, NS; The Chester Art Centre, Chester, NS; The Historic Gardens, Annapolis Royal, NS; private collections and many publications.

A juried Master Artisan of Craft Nova Scotia, she was a board member of the Canadian Crafts Council and is a member of the Art Gallery of Nova Scotia. She is a founding member and board member of the Chester Art Centre, Chester, NS.

BARBARA MENZIES

Barbara is a true "bi-coastal....

Although Barbara has lived on Vancouver Island for the past 45 years, she was born and raised in Nova Scotia and her heart never truly left. This hasn't been more apparent than in a year such as this when the additional anguish and tragedy felt by all Nova Scotians everywhere made her long for 'home'…for the music, the warmth of the people and that famous resilience!

"I would certainly not be the first to state that the arts offer channels for making sense of our world in unique and creative ways. My father was a great lover of reading, poetry and song lyrics, a passion that he passed on to me at an early age. I still turn to all three when I am in need of comfort and inspiration. The many challenges of 2020 have been accompanied by fear, grief, uncertainty and their mirror images: opportunities for hope, kindness and time for inner reflection."

PHILIP MOSCOVITCH

Philip Moscovitch is the author of *Adventures in Bubbles and Brine*, a book of Nova Scotia fermentation stories and recipes. *Moosewood Cookbook* author Mollie Katzen calls it "a beautifully written book – at once a travel memoir, a weave of personal histories, and an inspiring recipe collection." Philip's story "On the Rocks" appeared in the WindyWood anthology *Soundings*. Philip has an MFA in creative non-fiction from the University of King's College and is a regular contributor to regional and national publications, writing on subjects ranging from mental health to professional wrestling. In addition to writing, Philip is an audio producer and co-hosts the books podcast "Dog-Eared and Cracked."

CHAD NORMAN

Chad Norman lives beside the high tides of the Bay of Fundy, in Truro, Nova Scotia.

He has given talks and readings in Denmark, Sweden, Wales, Ireland, Scotland, America and across Canada.

Chad's poems appear in publications around the world and have been translated into Danish, Albanian, Romanian, Turkish, Italian, Spanish, Chinese and Polish. His collections are *Selected & New Poems* (Mosaic Press), and *Squall: Poems In The Voice Of Mary Shelley*, from Guernica Editions.

GLENDA JOY PENNELL

Glenda Joy grew up in Fairview and now lives in Fox Point, Nova Scotia. She is forever grateful to her mom Jessie, who instilled and nurtured the love of music by teaching her to play guitar and sing, then enrolling her in 7 years of classical piano lessons. Glenda Joy played in numerous bands of miscellaneous genres for close to 50 years. The love of music blossomed into passion when she started writing her own songs in 2005, which resulted in a CD of originals called *Muddy Water* released in 2018. She also wrote a theme song for Cove FM's radio soap opera called *Wild Cove*, a jingle for Ross Farm's Rural Roots Market and she continues to write new songs for her 2nd album. Her dream is that her music will do something good in the world – like warm hearts, touch souls, and connect spirits. As well as music, Glenda Joy also loves gardening, painting, jewellery-making, the ocean and her deepest love – her two boys, Ryan and Dylan.

LOUISE PIPER

Louise Piper was born in Canada to British parents and is a former teacher of English, having roamed the corridors and classrooms of UK high schools for many years. Eventually, her fun and creative side broke free and she committed to her writing full time. As part of this process, she gave up her teaching career, sold her house in England and relocated to Nova Scotia with the blessing of her grown-up daughter and son. Since arriving in Halifax, she has edited two McGill-Queen's University Press publications, *Canadian Justice, Indigenous Injustice* by Kent Roach and *Capitalism and the Alternatives* by Julius H. Grey.

Alongside her writing, Louise is currently a companion to a lady in a long-term care facility. Poetry is Louise's first love and she also enjoys comedy-sketch writing. Her first book, *The Year I Lived With a Psychic*, was published in October 2019. This book recounts the extraordinary adventure she had when she was invited to live and write with a psychic medium in Spain to help the psychic tell her story.

BRENT SEDO

Brent Sedo has spent more than 30 years as a freelance writer, publishing hundreds of articles in a variety of topics, and worked for more than a decade as a small press magazine editor in both Vancouver, BC and Halifax, NS.

He studied journalism at the University of North Dakota and is a graduate of the Simon Fraser University Creative Writing Workshop program. His fiction has appeared in the SFU anthology *Emerge* as well as *Prairie Fire* magazine. Born and raised near Winnipeg, MB, he and his wife now split their time between Simms Settlement, NS and San Agustinillo, Oaxaca, Mexico. He's grateful for the opportunity to have his work included in *Gathering In*.

BETHANA SULLIVAN

Poetry is a river rushing, a still pool, the ocean carrying her. Poetry is a song of her soul, coming through her from the earth, the water, the fire and the air. She lives on the wild Eastern Shore of Nova Scotia, her second home.

As a contemporary Celtic shaman, an expressive arts psychotherapist, an educator and artist her work is imbued with movement, music of word, body and sound, with the longing for each of us to become comfortable in our bodies, on the earth and with soul as we follow life's calling.

This is Bethana's second published poem with a third in the works. Currently she is writing a series of poems entitled "Poetry as Memoir."

This poem emerged as a response to the myriad of emotions and experiences evoked by the COVID-19 Pandemic in her and around her in her community. It gave voice to the strength of ancestral history and reminded her that joy always walks with sadness.

ALNOOR RAJAN TALWAR

Alnoor Rajan Talwar is a writer, poet and playwright whose passion for compassion, hope, peace and the unity of humanity permeates much of his work and life.

Coming from a multi-cultural background: born Muslim, raised by a Hindu, having a Jewish caregiver and business partner and now living in a predominantly Christian environment, even singing in a Christian choir, he has a very unique outlook on life and an insight that eludes most people.

Living with Multiple Sclerosis, plus having spent over three years recovering from a serious car accident through rehab, numerous therapies and challenges, he has an in-depth understanding of the difficulties of being physically challenged. Despite that, he continues to look to the future with hope, optimism and enthusiasm. No challenge is too big for him and despite his disability and challenges, he lives his life to the fullest.

He conducts meditation classes, hosts International students and teaches EAL both as a volunteer and at the Bridgetown Region Community School.

Heather D. Veinotte

Playwright and author Heather D. Veinotte has written and directed over twenty plays for stage and radio. Heather lives with her husband, Bruce, in West Northfield, a charming community on the South Shore of Nova Scotia. They have a son and daughter, two grandsons, a step-granddaughter and two granddoggers. She is currently working on her fifth novel *Before The Dawn*, a sequel to *Beyond The Mist*. Her other books include *The Mystery on Skull Island*, *Lonely Angels* and *Weeping Angels*. Heather enjoys spending time with her family, reading, flower arranging and watching British shows when she's not in the throes of writing. You can contact Heather by email: heatherdveinotte52@gmail.com

Deborah Washington

Of Newfoundland heritage, Deborah Washington, was born on the shores of Lake Ontario. In 2014 she swapped those waters to fulfill her dream of living beside the ocean.

With her partner, she moved to Lunenburg where she operated a successful art gallery and B&B for five years before closing in 2019.

Trained as a visual artist and chef, Deborah has been writing for the past decade, currently working on a collection of short stories and poems.

In spring 2020, Deborah completed a Creative Writing Diploma course at Memorial University in St. John's. Along with writing, Deborah enjoys playing her vintage accordion and strolling along the beautiful beaches of the South Shore.

MARY ANNE WHITE

Mary Anne White is a wife, mother, grandmother, researcher and writer, living in Halifax, Nova Scotia. She has spent more than 30 years as a professor of chemistry and physics at Dalhousie University. She is now is professor (emerita), and continues to do research in the areas of energy storage and sustainability. In addition to being a scientist, Mary Anne has been a dedicated promoter of the importance of science and scientific literacy, through interactions with the public – including 14 years as a regular guest on CBC Radio's *Maritime Noon*.

Mary Anne has received many honours, including Fellowship in the Royal Society of Canada, and induction as an Officer in the Order of Canada. She is author of a textbook *Physical Properties of Materials*, now in its third edition, and more than 200 research publications. This is her first creative writing piece, and it is slightly modified from "A Bride, A Groom and a Zoom Call," published in the "First Person" column in *The Globe & Mail* in 2020.

WindyWood Publishing

WindyWood Publishing is a small press featuring work by Nova Scotia writers and artists. It also supports local designers and photographers.

WindyWood Publishing is located in Simms Settlement, close to the vibrant community of Hubbards – about 30 minutes from Halifax.

For more than 80 years, Hubbards has been home to the Shore Club's famous lobster suppers.

Hubbards' Saturday Farmer's Market is ranked third in Canada. Close to Hubbards magical castles pop up, vacation rentals welcome, seascapes enthrall and waves and sea breezes roll in on ten sandy beaches.

To contact WindyWood Publishing:
Patricia Thomas
372 Highway #3, R.R. #1
Hubbards, N.S.

Telephone: 902-858-2030
Email: editpat001@gmail.com
https://www.patthomaseditor.com/windywood-publishing